How to Maintain a

Positive Cash Flow

How to Maintain a
Positive Cash Flow

A PRACTICAL NO-NONSENSE
GUIDE TO KEEPING YOUR
BUSINESS AFLOAT – AND YOUR
BANK MANAGER HAPPY

GILLIAN CLEGG

BUSINESS BOOKS LIMITED

Copyright © Gillian Clegg 1991

The right of Gillian Clegg to be identified as the author of this work has been asserted by her in accordance with the Copyright, Designs and Patents Act 1988

First published in 1991 in Great Britain by
Business Books Limited
An imprint of Random Century Limited
20 Vauxhall Bridge Road, London SW1V 2SA

Random Century Australia (Pty) Limited
20 Alfred Street, Milsons Point, Sydney
New South Wales 2061, Australia

Random Century New Zealand Limited
18 Poland Road, Glenfield
Auckland 10, New Zealand

Random Century South Africa (Pty) Limited
PO Box 337, Bergvlei, South Africa

Typeset by 𝍂 Tek Art Ltd, Addiscombe, Croydon, Surrey
Printed and bound in Great Britain by
Mackays of Chatham PLC, Chatham, Kent

British Library Cataloguing in Publication Data
A catalogue record for this book is available from the British Library

ISBN 0-09-174848-8 (hbk)
ISBN 0-09-174849-6 (pbk)

Contents

Foreword

Cash is the life blood of every business, irrespective of size and stage of development. Its management is of fundamental importance to all businesses and can be achieved only through effective planning and monitoring of resources. This enables difficulties which lie ahead to be anticipated and forces decisions to be made while there is still time to implement them.

Maintaining a positive cash flow is an integral part of the management of working capital and the control of financial risk. Just as much emphasis is required on the control and level of stocks of raw materials, components, work in progress and finished goods, as on debt collection from customers and payment policy to suppliers. All too often, when a business embarks on a period of profitable growth, it fails to plan for the cash impact of increasing levels of stocks and debtors, through higher turnover, and the need to make greater payments to staff and suppliers, ahead of the increasing flow of cash from customers and the conversion of profit into liquid resources.

Good housekeeping, including the control and reduction of costs, as well as effective policies for cash collection and disbursement, can speed up the cycle of cash through the business. This can lead to a reduction or elimination of a borrowing requirement or an increase in available funds. Skilled cash management will create increased confidence with suppliers, customers, banks and shareholders. It is all the more important when a business has to operate in an environment of economic uncertainty, variable exchange rates and high and volatile interest rates.

How to Maintain a Positive Cash Flow takes the business owner through the whole process of effective cash management. It deals with the setting of targets for cash, measuring performance and updating forecasts, keeping costs down, improving profitability, assessing potential customers, getting paid as well as trading abroad. For the uninitiated there is a chapter on raising money, highlighting the pitfalls as well as the requirements and expectations of bankers and outside investors. Finally, there is some advice about investing surplus cash, if only for a short period until it is needed again in the business.

Whether you are thinking of starting up your own business for the first time, or you have survived the critical early period of a new business and are contemplating growth, or current business conditions are causing you to run a much tighter operation, this book should increase your awareness and understanding of the need to manage your cash resources more effectively and your ability to achieve a positive cash flow.

Barry Baldwin
Director, Independent Business Services, Price Waterhouse
and Special Adviser to the Small Firms Minister, Department of Employment

Acknowledgements

Many thanks to Michael Barry, Lloyds Bank, Brian Mares, Michael Scully and Robert Troop for their help with the preparation of this book.

Thanks also to Colin Barrow, Her Majesty's Stationery Office, Intrum Justita, Lloyds Bank, Regency Consultants, The Solicitors's Law Stationery Society, Anthony Taylor and Trade Indemnity PLC for permission to reproduce their material.

Introduction

There are many reasons for going into business but only one real purpose – to make a profit. But although profit may be the name of the game, it is only by maintaining a positive cash flow that you can stay in the game long enough to win.

The glib answer to a business with cash flow problems is 'cut costs and stimulate sales', but these two courses are often incompatible since more sales usually mean more expenditure on stocks or materials, development and marketing which is counter-productive to cash flow since this expenditure is incurred long in advance of income received from sales.

Maintaining a positive cash flow is really all about running an efficient business. It starts with having systems in place to monitor activities, involves keeping costs down, profitability up, controlling payments and ensuring customers pay promptly. It's an exercise which embraces every aspect of a business – sales, stock, staff, purchases, premises, profit, creditors, customers, financiers.

Failure to balance the money coming in with the money flowing out is the rock on which too many businesses founder. The aim of this book is to make sure it doesn't happen to you. It's not an accountancy manual but a source of practical advice on the financial controls you need to ensure you stay on course; ways to keep expenditure down and maximize profits, and it addresses in some detail the perennial problem of extracting money from debtors. It provides guidance on what you can do if you discover you are under-financed, and when you are in the happy position of having surplus cash, how to turn this into even greater profit. Read it if you would rather swim than sink.

1

Are you going broke
without realizing it?

Cash is to business what blood is to a body: allow it to drain away
and the body becomes weak and eventually dies. The rapid
generation, conservation and effective utilization of cash is the
whole foundation on which a business rests. Business managers
thus need to ask themselves this question every single day of their
working lives: is the business running out of cash, and, if so, how
fast?

Can you answer this question for your business at this moment?
Unfortunately many business managers can't. Surveys on why
businesses fail consistently throw up insufficient grasp of financial
management as one of the major reasons businesses come to grief.
These businesses have often never analysed where they make or
lose money, nor have they set up the procedures and controls
which enable them to monitor what cash is coming into the
business, when, and how it balances with payments out.

Sadly, many of these firms appear, on the face of it, to be highly
successful. Sales are booming and profitability is high. What they
don't have, though, is the ready money to pay their day-to-day
bills. Their credit becomes exhausted and they perish. This is
called overtrading. It simply means that the business grows so fast
that it outstrips its financial resources. Although sales and profits
may be rising steadily, payments for materials and production
costs have to be made long before they produce money from
customers and the business has insufficient working capital to
bridge the cash-flow gap. To avoid the perils of overtrading you
should ensure you have raised enough long-term finance for the
projected sales you anticipate; otherwise trim your sales to the
amount of money available. And, of course, keep a close eye on

your cash flow situation using the financial controls described below.

Monitoring cash flow is not only essential for ensuring the survival of your business, but the consequences of not doing so can be pretty dire for you personally if your business goes to the wall. The Insolvency Act 1986 made it an offence for the director of a limited company to carry on trading when he/she 'knew, or ought to have known, that the company had no prospect of avoiding insolvency'. Directors who fall foul of the Act can be disqualified from running another business in the future, and may be made liable for the company's debts – thus negating the advantages of limited liability status. Sole traders and partners who go bankrupt stand to lose everything they own and will have difficulty obtaining credit or raising a mortgage.

All businesses are unfortunately susceptible to occasional liquidity crises, ie insufficient cash to pay the bills. Even those exercising good cash-management policies and techniques can be undermined by external economic and trading factors outside their control. When a cash crisis looms on the horizon, it's important to analyse the reason. Is it a cash flow problem, which is temporary and will be rectified shortly by more money being received? Or is it genuine illiquidity, ie lack of cash? All too often the business manager's knee-jerk reaction to a cash crisis is to seek a temporary cash injection – which often just postpones the day of reckoning – rather than investigating the underlying cause. If the liquidity crisis is due to basic unprofitability, the question that needs to be asked is: is the business worth saving? There is really no point in keeping alive a business that is terminally ill.

Monitoring company health

Your business no doubt produces some form of annual accounts – if a limited company it is, of course, required to do so by law. These accounts are essential for the long-term running of the business but they are well nigh useless for day-to-day monitoring of the company's health since they are not usually available until well into the following year, and if anything is amiss it is probably too late to put it right.

Businesses should know at the end of each month, if not every week, whether it has been a profitable one and whether there is enough money on hand, or on tap, to cover expenses for the coming week/month. This involves the preparation of some form of regular management accounts. They needn't be very elaborate but they should be produced in a form that managers can understand and act on.

Whether you get your accountant to prepare these for you, or prepare them yourself is up to you. It will considerably bump up the accountant's bill if he is asked to do it, and there is the danger that you may have trouble understanding his reports. On the other hand you may simply feel you lack the time for what is quite a time-consuming exercise. The argument for managers doing it themselves, though, is that they will become totally familiar with the state of the business at all times and thus more able to attempt to right the wrongs and forecast what is going to happen next. An accountant, after all, cannot compel you to look after your business health properly and he certainly can't cure a sickness that becomes terminal.

A satisfactory compromise adopted by many firms is to get an accountant who understands your particular requirements to devise a format for the regular accounts which you can then operate yourself.

Maintaining good business records – cash book, sales ledger, purchase ledger, general ledger etc – is a pre-requisite for compiling regular accounts. If yours aren't up to scratch, again, ask an accountant to give you some advice.

These are the regular statements it is sensible to have:

- **Profit and loss account** (see Figure 1). This should show cumulative totals for the past months of the current budgetary year, and a separate column for the current month – all actual figures should be compared with budgeted amounts. If this seems too time-consuming to prepare each month, a monthly trading account which omits fixed costs (which are usually for regular amounts anyway) will probably suffice. This shows your labour and material costs and the difference between the value of your opening and closing stocks. These are subtracted from your total monthly sales figures to show gross profit.

Figure 1 Profit and loss account

Period covered _____ 19 ____ to _____ 19 ____

Business name _____

Period (eg 4 weeks/Month)		BUDGET	ACTUAL	BUDGET	ACTUAL
SALES INCOME: Cash sales					
Credit sales					
TOTAL SALES INCOME	A				
DIRECT COSTS: Materials and services					
Other expenditure chargeable to customers (eg delivery costs)					
Commissions & discounts					
Productive wages and NI					
Other					
TOTAL DIRECT COSTS	B				
GROSS PROFIT (Total sales income less total direct costs A-B)	C				
OVERHEADS: Salaries and NI					
Rent, rates					
Heat, light and power					
Repairs and maintenance					
Bank charges and interest					
Insurance					
Legal and professional fees					
Stationery, postage and telephone					
Advertising and promotion					
Other overhead expenses					
Bad debts					
Depreciation					
TOTAL OVERHEADS	D				
PROFIT BEFORE TAX (Gross profit less total overheads C-D)					
TOTAL TO BRING FORWARD TO NEXT MONTH/PERIOD					

- **Net liquid assets statement** (see Figure 2). This shows the firm's liquid assets (cash in hand, in the bank, money owned by debtors) and the current liabilities (payments to creditors, current tax payments and other outgoings for the month).

Figure 2 Net liquid assets

LIQUID ASSETS   £
Cash in hand & at bank
Debtors
Other amounts currently
  receivable

           _____

TOTAL LIQUID ASSETS

Less: CURRENT LIABILITIES   £
Trade creditors
Provision for current tax
  Vat provision
Bank overdraft & loans
  currently payable
Other creditors & amounts
  currently payable

           _____

TOTAL CURRENT LIABILITIES

NET LIQUID ASSETS   £

- **Cash flow analysis.** All receipts and payments recorded by main headings on a weekly or monthly basis with a cash flow *forecast* (see page 19) for the next 12 months (at least).
- **Aged debtor analysis.** The money owed by customers arranged by age of the debt (see Chapter 5).
- **Aged creditor analysis.** Ditto for the people you have to pay (see Chapter 3).

You need these general regular statements as soon as possible after the period to which they refer – quick, roughly prepared statements are more useful than accurate, but slow-to-appear statements. But regular statements are no use at all unless the business managers take note of them. It is vital that the people running the business make time to sit down together regularly and discuss what these statements tell them.

Profit and loss account v. cash flow analysis

Don't make the mistake, as many business managers do, of running your business by the bottom line of the profit and loss account, or you could be in for a nasty shock if things start to go wrong. The P and L account measures profit for the period – but it's perfectly possible to be making a profit whilst running out of cash.

The reason for this is that the sales income, shown on the top line of the profit and loss account, is accounted for when the goods/service have been delivered and the invoice raised, which is usually very different from the time the payment is received. Therefore, the net profit shown on the bottom line may not be there for you to spend. This is illustrated by these simple accounts:

Table 1 Profit and loss account (one month)

	£
SALES	60,000
Cost of sales	30,000
GROSS PROFIT	30,000
LESS EXPENSES	
Rent and rates	5,000
Wages	10,000
Advertising	1,500
Other	4,800
Total	21,300
NET PROFIT	8,700

Seemingly, a perfectly respectable £8,700 profit for the month. However, the cash flow analysis which shows the money *actually* received from sales tells a very different story.

Table 2 Cash flow

	Week 1	Week 2	Week 3	Week 4
CASH IN				
Sales (A)	8,000	9,000	10,000	11,000
CASH OUT				
Purchases	5,000	6,000	7,000	8,000
Rent & rates	1,250	1,250	1,250	1,250
Wages	2,400	2,400	2,600	2,600
Advertising	250	250	500	500
Other	1,100	1,100	1,100	1,100
Total out (B)	10,000	11,000	12,450	13,450
Cash flow (A–B)	(2,000)	(2,000)	(2,450)	(2,450)

CUMULATIVE CASH FLOW (negative)

	(2,000)	(4,000)	(6,450)	(8,900)

This firm was really £8,900 out of pocket – a difference of £17,600 compared to the profit statement and a good example of why you need to monitor cash flow as well as profit.

Measuring performance

Using, and understanding, financial reporting and forecasting systems is essential for anyone controlling a business, but it goes further. You need also to be able to interpret and analyse what the figures are telling you. Fortunately, this can be done quite simply by the use of business ratios.

Ratios allow you to compare how your business is performing year-to-year (or month-to-month), and to compare your performance with that of other firms in the same line of business (not, though, with *any* other firm as different norms for different ratios apply). External financiers use ratios all the time to make objective assessments of the firms which approach them for finance and, since it is unlikely that you will never need to talk to a financier, it is sensible to understand how they measure the state of a business.

Here are some of the most useful ratios for monitoring cash flow:

- **The liquid ratio.** Often referred to as the 'acid test' or 'quick ratio', it indicates the firm's ability to meet its immediate commitments. It is calculated thus:

$$\frac{\text{Liquid assets}}{\text{Current liabilities}}$$

Liquid assets are the firm's cash, debtors and securities; current liabilities the trade creditors and other short-term liabilities.

As an example of how to work out and express ratios, assume the liquid assets are £50,000 and the current liabilities £30,000.

$$\text{Liquid ratio} = \frac{50,000}{30,000} = 1.6$$

This shows that current liabilities are covered 1.6 times and the ratio is expressed: 1.6:1. A ratio of 1:1 or more indicates good liquidity – it suggests the business can pay its immediate debts from short-term funds. Falling below 1:1, unless seen to be temporary, indicates a cause for concern and the possibility of an ongoing cash problem plus likely pressure from creditors seeking payment.

- **The current ratio.** This measures the amount of working capital available at a given time:

$$\frac{\text{Current assets}}{\text{Current liabilities}}$$

Current assets are the liquid assets mentioned in the previous section plus stock and work in progress, and since stock can't necessarily be turned into cash quickly, as an indicator of good liquidity this ratio needs to be higher than the liquid ratio – closer to 2:1 is the usual rule of thumb. This, though, will vary depending on the type of business – manufacturers with high stocks of raw materials and work in progress will operate at much higher ratios than retailers buying in finished goods on credit and selling them for cash – and between different businesses of the same type because of discrepancies in such things as asset purchases and length of the production cycle. This ratio is vital, though, for measuring your own performance over a period of time and is the ratio which alerts you to the dangers of overtrading (see page 5).

You need to have a positive cash flow *and* be profitable, of course, to survive long-term.

The **Return on Investment ratio** allows you to monitor the trends in profitability:

$$\frac{\text{Profit before tax}}{\text{Capital employed}}$$

Capital employed includes share capital, reserves and undistributed profits. The answer is expressed as a percentage, viz:

$$\text{ROI} = \frac{£100,000}{£750,000} = 13.3\%$$

This is the fundamental performance ratio, but profit before tax and capital employed can be further analysed by relating them to turnover:

$$\frac{\text{Profit before tax}}{\text{Turnover}} \qquad \frac{\text{Turnover}}{\text{Capital employed}}$$

● **Gearing ratio**. Another ratio which financiers always pay close attention to:

$$\text{Gearing ratio} = \frac{\text{debt capital}}{\text{net worth}}$$

This measures the proportion of the owners' or shareholders' funds (including both share capital and retained profits) to funds borrowed externally. The financier wants to be sure that the firm will be able to keep up the interest payments due on any further loan. A company with a very large proportion of borrowed money to equity of its own is considered highly geared and at risk of running into liquidity problems since interest has to be paid whether or not the company is making profits. Research into the failure of businesses borrowing under the Government's Loan Guarantee Scheme suggests that a gearing greater than 4:1 is nearly always fatal.

There are many more useful ratios as well as those mentioned above; you will find others scattered throughout the following chapters under the subjects to which they relate.

When using ratios for your business, bear in mind that it is essential to compare like with like. The information on which the ratios are based should be calculated identically each time, so if your accounting methods or presentation change, or your method of trading, then the comparisons over a period could be misleading.

Different methods of preparation can be a problem too when comparing your ratios with those of a similar company – but there is little you can do about this except to accept that ratios are just a guide and not hard and fast facts. Many credit reporting services supply ratios in the credit status reports (see Chapter 4) they prepare on individual companies, which is one way to discover how your competitors are doing.

If you want to discover how you measure up within your particular business sector, see if your trade association or trade magazines have the relevant data, or it may be contained in official statistics or published surveys in financial newspapers/magazines.

You might also like to know about two organizations which specialize in information containing ratios. ICC Business Ratios (see Appendix A) produces 196 reports on different business sectors which analyse the performance of UK companies in each sector, using a number of different ratios. At the time of writing (1990) reports costs £225 each.

The Centre for Interfirm Comparison (see Appendix A), an independent company under the auspices of the British Institute of Management and the British Productivity Council, will help businesses of every kind to assess their performance and then take steps to improve it. You can use the Centre on a consultancy basis to design you a tailor-made set of ratios by which to measure your business generally and perhaps to compare different departments within the business. The Centre also runs regular inter-firm comparisons whereby participating firms feed a range of information to the Centre which then produces a report showing how the firms compare by the use of around 100 different ratios. Since the Centre directs the participants on the information to be provided, the results are truly comparable and enable participants to evaluate their strengths and weaknesses. All information is provided on a totally confidential basis and no one firm is identified in the report. The reports are not available to non-participating companies. It should be said, however, that the Centre doesn't cover very many business sectors.

Setting targets

It is amazing how many businesses, even those that are long-established with a considerable turnover, don't draw up any budgets or make any plans at all for their short or long-term future – they just sit back and react to what each day brings.

Even businesses that do prepare annual budgets often begrudge the time it takes to review past results and prepare future plans, many feeling this exercise is purely for the benefit of the accountant so that he can calculate his overhead rate for the coming year and make some tentative guesses at the finance required.

But a business without overall goals and objectives is like a rudderless ship, at the mercy of all the winds and tides of chance and change. Forward planning is thus a necessary and healthy management function. It gives you the opportunity of considering how you can develop sales, reduce costs, improve efficiency and so increase your profits, which is after all the name of the game.

Having budgets and forecasts against which actual results are regularly compared also allows you to see trouble looming up some time ahead and enables you to take remedial action before the trouble becomes a crisis.

There are three aspects to forward planning: the setting of long-term goals for the business and its shareholders, the preparation of budgets and the preparation of forecasts.

Long-term plans

Planning for more than a year ahead is considered something of a luxury by many firms. But there's nothing like having long-term targets to shoot at to stimulate effort (see the case story on page 16).

A business that knows where it's going can use its resources more effectively and exploit market opportunities which it might otherwise have missed by not looking far enough ahead. Knowing your long-term goals also makes day-to-day decisions easier because you have a plan to refer to.

When planning long-term, the objectives you set should be clear and specific: 'We want sales to top £100,000 in two years' time', or, 'We aim to achieve ten per cent return on capital by 1995', rather than 'We aim to improve profits in the next three years'.

Work out how you can begin to achieve these goals using the SWOT analysis, ie determining your business's *strengths* and *weaknesses*, and recognizing the *opportunities* and *threats* you face. This is how it might read for a small company manufacturing special machines:

STRENGTHS:	Innovation
	Low overheads
	Financial security
WEAKNESSES:	Poor office facilities
	Insufficient knowledge of the market
	Owner-managed and vulnerable
OPPORTUNITIES:	Hire (rather than sell) machines
THREATS:	Increased competition
	Progressive reduction in margins.

Once you've carried out this exercise you should be in a better position to outline the path your company should take to achieve the objectives set. But do remember, objectives and plans are not cast in stone, re-appraise them annually, particularly if economic and market conditions change significantly.

Case Story 1

How setting a target stimulated this company's profits

One components company doubled its turnover and tripled its profits in three years by the simple device of deciding to go on the Unlisted Securities Market (USM).

The business had been jogging along quite comfortably for nearly ten years, making profits of anywhere between £20,000 and £60,000. The managers always felt the business could be

---

more successful but they never bothered to find the time to sit down and work out exactly how.

Then one day a friendly accountant suggested the managers should think of floating the business on the USM. If they could establish a reasonable profit graph over three years, say, £80,000, £140,000 and £200,000, he told them, they might float the company at a value of perhaps £1 million.

The managers weren't entirely convinced that this was a good idea but they decided to aim for it anyway.

The effects were amazing. Suddenly the managers had a target to shoot at and everyone knew where they were going. Not only did the managers sit down for the first time and work out a plan to achieve the goals but they also became much more efficient. They did all the sensible things they'd never got round to such as cutting out unprofitable lines, chasing slow payers more diligently, getting rid of free-loading staff, and as a result hit the profit targets without too much sweat.

As it happens the business never did go on the USM, but it had the same effect in the end.

Budgets

Budgets are the expression of your annual plan in cash and trading terms and actual results are always compared against budgeted results as the year progresses. This means the budgets become part of the management's means of control and measurement of the performance of the business.

Big companies draw up budgets for every department and every aspect of their activities. Smaller companies probably don't need to be quite so sophisticated but should consider annual budgeting for such things as cost of materials, turnover, gross profit, wages and salaries, research and development, rent and rates, administrative overheads, marketing and promotional activities. It is also worth budgeting stock levels and debtor levels on a monthly basis, reflecting the trend of sales through the year.

Budgets which set achievable goals have the additional value that they stimulate everyone to keep to the targets. But it's not always easy to predict a year ahead, and if, because of unforeseen changes in the business environment, the budgets become unattainable, they are in danger of being disregarded; if they are too easy to achieve they are useless as a standard.

Budgets thus need to be prepared carefully and reviewed regularly. Having said that, smaller firms should also be prepared to ditch their budgets altogether if new opportunities come along which should be grabbed straight away, or if they find they're in bad trouble. The high degree of flexibility small firms have to change course rapidly to exploit new openings or avoid a looming disaster is one of their main advantages over their larger brethren.

Forecasts

Forecasts are conceptually different from budgets. They are the best estimate, the best guess, of future performance. They can be prepared for long periods ahead, or for short periods like a month or a week. Because they are only assumptions they are not considered as binding on a business as budgets, but if actual results are way below forecasted results something is very wrong and action needs to be taken.

The one vital bit of forecasting every business keen to stay afloat needs to do is the cash flow forecast. This should be prepared for every month for the next 12 months at least (financiers often require cash flow forecasts for the next few years too). If your business is hanging on by the skin of its teeth, consider forecasting cash flow every week – this gives you 52 opportunities to take corrective action, rather than just 12.

If you haven't prepared a cash flow forecast before this step-by-step guide will help you.

- **Forecasting sales**. Before you start on the cash flow forecast itself you must estimate your likely sales for the periods in question. It's no good saying, as some managers do, that sales can't be predicted. They *must* be predicted, on reasonable and cautious grounds, if you are going to have any control over your finances.

  Methods commonly used are a combination of the experiences of previous years, orders in hand, the opinion of your salesforce, market research and statistical techniques – many microcomuter software packages incorporate statistical functions to aid sales forecasting.

- **Receipts**. Now you can start to forecast cash flow. If your customers buy on credit rather than cash, when will you get paid for the sales made in a particular month? Much will

ARE YOU GOING BROKE WITHOUT REALIZING IT?

Figure 3 Cash flow forecast

Period (eg 4 weeks/Month)		BUDGET	ACTUAL
RECEIPTS			
Cash sales			
From debtors			
Other income (eg from capital introduced)			
TOTAL RECEIPTS	A		
PAYMENTS			
Cash purchases			
To creditors			
Wages/salaries/NI/Other			
Rent/Rates			
Light/heat/power			
Maintenance			
Advertising & promotion			
Professional fees			
Stationery, postage and telephone			
Other expenses			
Bank/finance charges & interest			
HP payments/leasing charges			
Insurance			
Drawings/dividends			
VAT-net			
Tax			
Loan repayments			
Capital expenditure			
TOTAL PAYMENTS	B		
A-B (net inflow) or B-A (net outflow)	C		
Bank balance at end of previous period brought forward	D		
Bank balance at end of period carried forward (aggregate of C + D)			
Agreed overdraft			

depend on your credit terms, speed of invoicing and your experience of slow payers. It may, for example, be realistic to assume that January receipts will consist of half the sales invoiced in the preceding December and half those invoiced in November. Don't forget to take into account any large customers with whom you've negotiated special terms, firms likely to take a discount for prompt payment – if you offer one – and allow for bad debts.

Other receipts which you may or may not have in the period include interest or dividends receivable from trade or other investments, and receipts from the sale of fixed assets, or even perhaps from selling off part of your business.

- **Payments.** Many of these can usually be forecast with great accuracy: wages, salaries, National Insurance, pension contributions, rates, rent, electricity, lease or rental payments on equipment, income tax or Corporation Tax, since you know the due dates and the approximate amounts of payment.

The sales forecast will determine the amount of materials or stock bought in any period and the variable overheads, also the amount of VAT to be paid. Major asset purchases (machinery, equipment etc) and repayments of loan capital need to be included. Interest due and proprietors' drawings or dividends should be the last items to be assessed, on the basis of the cash position shown by the forecast.

When compiling a cash flow forecast, it's sensible to project likely receipts from sales pessimistically, so as to discount the natural optimism of sales executives and, indeed, many managers. Conversely, expected payments out should be overstated rather than understated, and contingencies included to cover unexpected expenses.

Once the forecast has been compared with actual monthly (or weekly) figures it should be revised in the light of the real totals, and re-projected forward for the next 12 or so months. In this way your ability to forecast will improve steadily and the figures will become increasingly more accurate and therefore more useful to you.

If the forecasts show a temporary cash shortage is likely to develop in, say, the next six months, you need to take immediate action because you could become insolvent even in that short period, or at least have to restrict your activities severely. The first course of action is to obtain or increase temporary finance such as your bank overdraft (alert your bank manager in good time). Next, to improve procedures for getting your money in from debtors. If the forecasts indicate a short-term surplus, then short-term investments should be made (see Chapter 9).

2

Keeping costs down

Controlling costs is one activity that's almost totally within your own governance, and not dependent on the whims of the marketplace. And so many different costs are involved in running a business that it only needs a couple of percentage points shaved off each cost area to give you a fairly substantial cost reduction overall. That's money you can use for working capital now, or hold in reserve to cushion you against possible bad times ahead.

If the Department of Energy is right, businesses use 20 per cent more fuel than they need, so you can almost certainly make savings in energy use. If business consultants are right, there is 20 per cent too much slow-moving or redundant stock in your stockroom (if you have one), and if your staff go in for petty pilfering in terms of fiddles on expenses and telephone abuse or mis-use, you can surely tighten up on that. You might not be able to get your rent or rates reduced but at least you'll have an idea whether it is possible after reading this chapter.

Conserving cash is of prime importance to many businesses, which is why it often makes sense to rent or lease assets, rather than purchase them outright. And when you do need to consider making a capital investment purchase, it is essential to assess whether it is really going to be worthwhile by estimating the additional income it will produce and the additional outgoings that will be incurred (this is explained later in this chapter).

Always remember that the availability of an overdraft facility may well ease the pressure which continued good housekeeping might achieve without it, controlling the need for working capital and eliminating the requirement of an overdraft.

Acquiring assets

Purchasing assets – office machines, vehicles etc – outright makes large holes in your valuable capital which could almost certainly be put to better use funding future growth.

The alternatives to outright purchase are to hire machinery etc on a short-term basis; to buy goods by a lease-purchase/industrial hire purchase agreement or to rent goods by leasing.

It should be said that it is unlikely to be cheaper in the long run to acquire your assets by these methods but it certainly frees up your cash which may be needed for increasing working capital requirements as the business expands. It's a question of balancing the various demands on your cash resources.

The alternatives to outright purchase include:

- **Short-term hire.** This speaks for itself and is useful for equipment such as scaffolding, skips, tractors and other equipment required for a specific job.
- **Lease-purchase or industrial hire purchase.** This means you pay for the goods by instalments (usually over a period of two to five years) and they become your property at the end of the period. The rental payments are, however, treated as capital instalments for tax purposes so you are entitled to claim an annual writing down allowance on the purchase price.
- **Leasing.** This is quite different from lease-purchase in that the goods never belong to you. Technically, they always remain the property of the leasing company, so leasing is really just an agreement to rent goods. But leasing is very popular and has grown by leaps and bounds over the last ten years – to the extent that now around 20 per cent of all equipment acquired in the UK is leased. And practically anything can be leased – cars, computers, machine tools, shop fittings, aeroplanes, oil rigs.

  It is also fairly complicated in that there are different types of lease agreement and variants within each type. The two main types of lease are the *finance lease* and the *operating lease*. There are several distinctions between them, perhaps the main one being that, from 1987, equipment subject to a finance lease is required to be capitalized on your company balance sheet while that on an operating lease is not.

However, you will be required to disclose operating lease obligations in the notes to your annual accounts, so that people reading the accounts can see the full extent of your leasing obligations.

- *Finance leasing* is the cheapest form of leasing. A contract is made for a 'primary period' which depends on the expected useful life of the asset being leased. Normally, it is for four or five years but it can be as short as two years or as long as ten or more, depending on the particular piece of equipment. You have unrestricted use of the asset and are responsible for maintaining and insuring it.

  During this primary period the leasing company will expect to recover the full capital cost of the asset and a finance charge from the rental payments, which means that when the primary period is over, you usually have the option to take out a secondary lease at a much reduced rent, or the equipment can be sold to an unrelated third party. This is commonly arranged by the lessee, acting as agent for the leasing company, and the lessee then retains the bulk of the proceeds of the sale (by way of a rental rebate).

- *Operating leasing.* The leasing company doesn't anticipate recovering the whole of the capital investment from primary lease rental payments – it relies on getting a good price for the asset on the second-hand market to make up the difference. So operating leases are common for such things as vehicles, computers and aircraft where there is a viable second-hand market.

  Operating leases are thus usually for shorter periods (two years or so) than finance leases and are more expensive since the leasing company, wishing to protect the value of its asset, assumes responsibility for repair, maintenance and insurance.

- **Contract hire.** This is a form of operating lease used for fleets of motor vehicles which is fast gaining in popularity. As the hirer, you rent the car(s) for a fixed period, usually three years or an earlier completion of, say, 45,000 miles after which the leasing company sells it. The beauty of contract hire is that the leasing company virtually acts as your car fleet manager, saving you the hassle and repair bills of keeping cars on the road – leasing companies usually supply replacement vehicles should the hired vehicles break down – and you don't need to worry about depreciation when the second-hand market becomes depressed, or if the vehicles in question suffer particularly vigorous use.

As well as releasing capital for other uses, leasing makes it much easier to forecast your cash flow. Most (but not all) leasing agreements have the rental payments fixed at the outset and these can't be changed for any reason during the length of the agreement so you know precisely what to budget for where that particular asset is concerned.

Many leases, too, can be negotiated on tailor-made terms – businesses with seasonal demand, for instance, can have the rental pattern matched to the expected cash flow variations related to the earning power of the asset. Variants such as *balloon* rental push the bulk of the lease rental payments towards the end of the primary rental period so that they are virtually extinguished by the residual second-hand price.

Now for the downside. It is unlikely that the total cost of leasing an asset for four years or so will work out cheaper than purchasing it outright now. However, this is only one of the several calculations you need to make when choosing between leasing and buying (see Figure 4).

Also, because a leased asset never actually belongs to you, you can't claim the 25 per cent writing down allowance which you would if you bought the asset outright. The leasing company claims that, and it is precisely because it needs to protect its entitlement to this allowance that you can never buy the asset. Losing the writing down allowance won't matter of course if you pay little or no Corporation Tax, and you can deduct the rental payments from profits for tax purposes (the deductible amount is restricted in the case of cars costing more than £8,000).

It is expensive to cancel. When you take out a lease you are entering into a legally binding contract for a set period and the penalties for cancelling before the due date are very high, often almost as much as the remaining rental repayments. The one situation where the leasing companies are more reasonable regarding cancellation is when you are prepared to upgrade your equipment by taking out another (more expensive) lease for a superior machine from the same source.

The golden rule with leasing is to get the right goods for the right amount of time. Don't, for instance, lease a photocopier designed for a low volume of copying for three years now, if you hope and anticipate that your business growth will mean you are copying twice the amount in two years' time – it will be more trouble than it's worth. Short operating leases are obviously the sensible choice for areas where there is likely to be turbulent technological change – fax machines, computers etc.

Leasing companies are mainly subsidiaries of the banks, finance houses and insurance companies, although some product manufacturers have their own leasing operations. It is a very competitive industry so do shop around and compare the different deals offered once you have selected the machine you require. The representative body for leasing is The Equipment Leasing Association (address in Appendix A) which operates a code of practice to which members are obliged to conform. The ELA can supply a list of members and an informative free booklet on the different aspects of leasing.

Figure 4 Lease or purchase?

This simplified worked example assumes an asset with a useful life of five years, a purchase price of £20,000, a residual value of £4,746, or an annual rental of £7,000 (including finance charges). The figures are net of VAT. The writing down allowance for tax purposes is 25 per cent and the Corporation Tax rate for small companies, 25 per cent. The writing down allowance would reduce tax payments approximately a year after the allowance applied. For purposes of comparison, the outgoings for both purchase and leasing have been reduced by the respective tax reliefs.

Payments need to be discounted to reflect present day values (see page 42) so the net costs have been discounted by 15 per cent on the basis that this is a fairly normal borrowing rate for many businesses and it has been assumed that the same rate is charged by the leasing company in the rentals.

Here is the calculation for purchase with the writing down allowances:

Year		Cost & written down Balance	Capital allowance at 25%	Tax at 25%	Year effective
0		£20,000			
1	less 25%	5,000	5,000	1,250	2
		£15,000			
2	less 25%	3,750	3,750	937	3
		£11,250			
3	less 25%	2,813	2,813	703	4
		£8,437			
4	less 25%	2,109	2,109	527	5
		£6,328			
5	less 25%	1,582	1,582	395	6
		£4,746	£15,254	3,812	

Here is the comparison with leasing (tax relief at 25 per cent is deducted from the rentals to give an annual net cost of £5,250, and for simplicity the rentals are given as yearly payments – monthly payments would slightly increase the present value shown below).

		Purchase			Lease	
Year	Cost	Discount factor	Present value	Cost	Discount factor	Present value
0	£20,000	–	20,000	–	–	–
1	–	–	–	5,250		17,572
2	(1,250)	0.7561	(945)	5,250		
3	(937)	0.6575	(616)	5,250		
4	(703)	0.5718	(402)	5,250	3.3472	
5	(527)	0.4972	(262)	5,250		
6	(395)	0.4323	(171)			
	(4,746)	0.4323	(2,052)			
	£11,442		15,552	26,250		17,572

This calculation does not, however, take into account the amount of profit foregone on the cash used to purchase the asset (ie how much money that £20,000 would have made for you if used for other things or invested). If it was as much as 20 per cent, though, and the figures were discounted at that rate, the present value of purchasing, rather than leasing, would still be lower than the present value of leasing.

In this particular example, it is thus more economic to purchase than to lease and you'll find this is often the case, although each project requires separate calculation. Leasing, however, is simpler administratively, especially contract hire for cars, and is the obvious recourse where capital for purchasing assets is not readily available and needs to be conserved for expansion.

Challenging a rent rise

Leases on commercial properties almost invariably contain built-in provisions for regular rent reviews, and, unless the lease states otherwise, the landlord has *carte blanche* to demand any figure he likes. Frequently this can be a massive rise – double or more is not uncommon.

Commercial tenants, unfortunately, don't have the same legal safeguards as residential tenants who can immediately apply to a rent tribunal to fix a 'fair' rent. It is assumed that businesses have the funds to seek legal advice and pursue a settlement through negotiation and, if necessary, arbitration.

When you receive a rent review, look immediately at the terms of your lease. It may specify how long you have in which to debate the review, and failure to acknowledge the review, or submit a counter-claim within a set time limit, may be tantamount to accepting the rent suggested. Conversely, the timing may work to your advantage. If the landlord fails to send out his notice by the date indicated in the lease he may forfeit his right to the review.

See, also, if the lease contains a clause agreeing to settlement by arbitration in the event of a dispute. If not, and you are unable to negotiate a settlement with the landlord direct, you may have to get a court order to go to arbitration.

Decide next whether the rent asked is reasonable given the property's current value on the open market. First, are you paying the right sum for the right amount of space? Commercial rents are normally quoted on a square footage basis and a slip of the tape measure could result in you paying for more space than you occupy. Check exactly how much square footage you have.

How does the rent compare with similar properties in the area? Talk to estate agents and other tenants and compile a list of rentals for similar accommodation. Although no two offices or shops are identical, this exercise should provide some useful guidelines. Bear in mind, though, that with some types of business, size and condition are probably less important than a key location.

Are there any plans in the pipeline for road closures, one way streets, or other work which may affect the value of the property – and harm your business? Try to discover. And, if the landlord offers what appears to be an extremely reasonable rent increase, check it out – he may know something you don't. Staff on the local paper and tame councillors are good contacts to have.

Once you have gathered your evidence and you think you have a case, start negotiating. You can do this on your own, or, if you prefer, use a solicitor or chartered surveyor to do battle on your behalf.

It is often sensible to involve a solicitor at the outset, to interpret the lease, tell you the relevant case law and generally advise you how to proceed. Some leases, though, make the tenant responsible for both the tenant's legal fees *and* the landlord's which could make the exercise expensive if you anticipate a long fight.

Chartered surveyors act as negotiators for hundreds of business tenants every year. The advantage of using one is that he knows the market, the relevant legislation and how to go about it. He will determine a fair rent then negotiate with the landlord to reach a settlement. He will either charge you a flat fee or a percentage of the final rent decided. Make sure you agree the basis of this fee in writing at the outset.

If agreement with the landlord can't be reached, the case can be determined by an arbitrator, or independent valuer, who will listen to both sides and make an independent assessment. This has force in law. The Royal Institution of Chartered Surveyors (see Appendix A) can help you find both a surveyor to act for you, and someone to arbitrate.

There will be a further fee for arbitration. This is usually split between landlord and tenant, and the arbitrator normally insists on payment before decisions are reached or awards made.

If you share a building with other tenants whose rents are coming up for review at the same time, see if they are prepared to join forces to fight the increases together. Your collective muscle will give you much greater bargaining power. And, if you take professional advice, you should be able to negotiate a group fee which will be lower than what you pay on your own.

Negotiating a rates reduction

'Taxes are paid in sorrow and rates in anger,' quipped some sage or other, and surveys of small businesses have consistently identified rates as one of the most crippling expenses they have to bear.

Before 1990 business rates were set by local authorities, so the amount paid by businesses in similar properties varied dramatically from area to area – many felt this was unfair since business rate-payers, having no vote, were unable to control the activities of free-spending councils. The introduction of the Uniform Business Rate in 1990 meant that businesses were no longer dependent on the whim of their particular local authority: the business rate is now set by central government and is the same per pound of rateable value for all businesses in England. Different rates apply to all businesses in Wales and in Scotland.

The Conservative Government has pledged itself to raise the rate by no more than the rate of inflation each year. The Labour Party, however, intends to get rid of the UBR and revert to something like the old rating system with the business rate being set locally.

You can't of course appeal against the UBR itself, but then you never were able to appeal against your rates bill per se. All you can – and ever could – challenge is the *rateable value* given to the premises you operate from.

Before 1990 you could do so whenever you felt you had a case, but since the introduction of the UBR, appeals can only be made six months after each property revaluation, which means that if you didn't appeal before 30 September 1990, you will have to wait until the next property review, which is scheduled for 1995, except in certain circumstances (see below).

The rateable value is based on the amount of rent the property could be let for on the open market at the time of the property valuation. The reason why rateable values – and therefore rates – increased so dramatically for many businesses when the UBR was introduced was because the property revaluation carried out in 1988 was the first since 1973 and rents, taking the country as a whole, had increased eight-fold during that period.

If you feel your rateable value is higher than it should be, it is certainly worth considering an appeal since it is unlikely that the Valuation Officer 'viewed' your premises – the rateable value given to them will most likely have been based on the general increase in rents in the area.

Why and when you can appeal

These are some of the grounds on which you can bring an appeal:

- Rateable value in excess of rental value as at the date of the property revaluation.
- Your rateable value is higher than that of similar premises nearby.
- Old and outdated premises, not particularly suitable for carrying on business.
- Difficulties in access to your premises by road, footpath etc for members of the public, deliveries and essential services.
- Interference from noise, dust, smell from nearby properties.

If you are taking over as the new occupier of a property, you can make an appeal on these grounds in between property revaluations, so long as you do so within six months of moving in, and so long as previous occupiers haven't done so and reached a decision with the Valuation and Community Charge Tribunal (your local Valuation Officer will be able to tell you if this has happened).

If you are an existing occupier you will have to wait until the next property revaluation to make your appeal *unless* certain changes have taken place. These are the reasons listed by the Department of the Environment for making an appeal between valuations, but bear in mind that all appeals must be made within six months of the event to which they relate:

- If the Valuation Officer notifies you that your entry in the rating list has been changed. This could happen if the property has been altered or improved in some way.
- If the property has been affected by what is termed 'a material change of circumstance'. This could be:
  - a change in its physical state, such as building an extension or demolition of a building
  - a change in the way the building is used

31

- a physical change in the locality, ie the introduction of a one-way road system, new parking restrictions, road closures etc
- a change in the use of neighbouring property.
- If the local Valuation and Community Charge Tribunal or the Lands Tribunal or a higher court reach a decision which has a bearing on the valuation of the property.

You, the occupier, are not the only person who can propose a change in the rateable value of the property. Your landlord can also do so, and if he does you will be notified and given the opportunity of taking part in the settlement or appeal. Local councils can also make proposals in relation to any properties in the area.

If you are considering an appeal on the grounds that changes have taken place in your trading area, your chances of winning will be increased if you put in a joint claim with neighbouring businesses blighted by the same problem.

How to appeal

To make a proposal to have your rateable value altered, you contact your local Inland Revenue Valuation Office (address in the phone book) which will send you a form on which you give the reasons why you believe the rating list entry is inaccurate, and what sort of change you wish to see. The Valuation Officer considers your proposal and, if he agrees, alters the entry.

If you and the Valuation Officer don't reach an agreement within six months of making the proposal, the matter is referred to the Valuation and Community Charge Tribunal, an independent body set up to resolve unsettled rating and community charge appeals. Commonly, the VCCT reaches a decision on the basis of written representations from you and the Valuation Officer.

If any of the parties don't agree that the case should be resolved by written representations, there will be a hearing. This is quite informal and both you and the Valuation Officer will have the opportunity to make a statement and ask questions. If you are dissatisfied with the decision reached by the Tribunal you have the right to appeal to the Lands Tribunal.

There is no charge for appealing to the VCCT but neither can the Tribunal award any costs, so you have to foot the bill for preparing the case, attending the hearing and for any expenses incurred in employing someone to help you.

Like challenging a rent rise (see page 29), the people to use to appeal on your behalf are chartered surveyors.

Just one point to bear in mind if you are contemplating an appeal: in 1990, for the first time, Valuation Tribunals were given the power to increase, as well as reduce, assessments on appeal!

Energy saving tips

British businesses use 20 per cent more energy than they need, says the Department of Energy, and this is an area where you can almost certainly find ways to cut costs with very little effort.

What's more it is also an area where there is plenty of free help available: the Department of Energy's Energy Efficiency Office produces a stack of useful booklets; free advice and information on all aspects of energy efficiency is available from your regional Department of Trade and Industry's Energy Efficiency Officer, and commercial energy consultants will often work for no fee, taking instead a percentage of the costs they save (so sure are they of getting results!) The local Electricity Councils also offer a free advisory service, and firms which make fantastic or ingenious savings using electricity may win cash prizes through the Electricity Council's Annual Awards Scheme.

But let's start with the basics: do you check your energy bills properly? Many companies don't pay nearly so much attention to bills from public utilities as they do to bills from suppliers. They assume they must be correct but this isn't necessarily so – accounts can be muddled by human error, meters can be misread, or, more seriously, meters may not be measuring accurately. It's worth taking a few minutes to scrutinize the bills and to check the billed number of units consumed against your own reading.

Gas meters are not always reliable, surveys have shown. If you have an old gas meter and feel you are being overcharged, ask your regional gas board to check it. There is a charge for this, but if the meter is out by more than a certain percentage either way, the charge is waived and backdated refunds may be given.

Electricity meters are generally very accurate, but if you are in doubt you can check the meter yourself against a known load, like a one kilowatt bar fire – making sure you switch *everything* else off first. Do take the trouble to investigate the different tariffs and ensure you are on the right one for your usage.

Energy efficiency

Energy use, and thus costs, can be managed just as finance, staff and other aspects of the business are managed. One senior member of staff needs to be given the responsibility for energy and assured of top-level backing. The first stage in implementing an energy programme is to carry out an 'Energy Audit'. This identifies the sums spent on energy and shows where and how the money goes – thus highlighting the areas with the greatest potential for savings.

The Energy Efficiency Office produces a step-by-step guide: *Fuel Efficiency I Energy Audits* which could prove invaluable for those who decide to carry out the audit in-house. But it's here where you might prefer to use an outside expert who knows the ropes.

How energy efficient are you compared with other offices, shops, factories etc? An interesting piece of information to discover and you can do so quite easily by following the instructions in the Energy Efficiency Office's *Energy Efficiency in Buildings* series (there is a separate booklet for each building type – shops, offices, hotels, factories etc). The booklets show you how to calculate your 'performance indicator' and provide yardsticks by which to measure whether your energy consumption is good, fair, or poor.

Once you know how you use energy, you can institute a programme to monitor consumption levels and set targets to progressively reduce consumption. By applying a formal budgeting procedure, fuel costs aren't just written off as unavoidable overheads but controlled like other budgeted costs.

Fuel saving measures

Energy efficiency starts, of course, with the design of the building itself, but the power to improve energy management systems here lies in the hands of planners, architects, developers and landlords for whom energy running costs weren't, or aren't, a priority. Buildings can be updated but this is likely to be more expensive than insulating the existing structure.

However, vast energy savings can be made by instituting simple 'good housekeeping' measures, which cost nothing, or by investing in improvements which should pay for themselves in the savings on energy bills.

Ways to save money in different types of business operation and different types of building obviously vary, but here are some tips for the energy areas common to all businesses:

LIGHTING

- Make sure all lights are turned off when not required.
- Make sure lamps and luminaires are regularly cleaned and maintained so that they provide optimum light.
- Fit automatic light switches to intermittently used areas – store rooms, staircases etc.
- For security lighting, consider using time switches, or automatic lighting controls which work either by sensitivity to light (the light comes on at dusk and off at dawn) or sensitivity to sound (the light comes on in response to noise, the sound of someone breaking in, say), or passive infrared lights which switch on when the sensor detects a combination of body heat and movement.
- Use the most efficient source of lighting (eg fluorescent rather than tungsten).

DOORS AND WINDOWS

- Keep outside doors and windows shut.
- Fit draught-proofing to external doors and windows which open.

SPACE HEATING

- Don't heat empty rooms.
- Don't overheat your premises – statutory minimum is 16°C and statutory maximum, 19°C.
- Check thermostats are set correctly.
- Don't leave heating on all night in winter.
- Use frost-protection thermostats outside working hours.
- Consider installing more accurate thermostats and thermostatic radiator valves (tamperproof types).
- Fit time controls to heating plant.
- Improve thermal insulation of boiler and pipework.

- If you have other sources of power, refrigerators, ventilation systems, for example, investigate whether it wouldn't be worth utilizing the heat recovered from these sources for space heating.

WATER HEATING

- Reduce the temperature to which water is heated.
- Install spray taps to keep water consumption down.
- Insulate hot water storage tanks and pipework.
- Consider point-of-use water heaters instead of central plant.

Fantastic savings in fuel consumption are claimed for even some of the simplest of these measures – turning down the space heating thermostat by just 2°C, for example, can reduce consumption by some 20 per cent.

For more information on fuel-saving devices in your particular type of business, and on energy efficiency generally, contact the Energy Efficiency Office (see Appendix A) for details of their publications.

Consultants

Expert energy management consultants frequently boast of slashing energy bills by margins as big as 40 per cent, which is why some consultants don't charge a fee for the consultancy work but formally agree with the client that they will split the energy cost savings in the first year 50/50. Other consultants charge a straight fee, or a daily rate.

To find the name of an independent and established energy management consultancy, contact the Energy Systems Trade Association (address in Appendix A).

Keeping stock under control

Business consultants claim that as much as 20 per cent of the money many firms have tied up in stock could be released to fund working capital or an expansion plan, since much of the stock companies hold is increasingly obsolete or slow moving in relation to potential demand.

In an ideal world, speedy manufacturing and rapid, regular deliveries would obviate the need to hold large quantities of raw materials, work in progress and finished goods. Many Japanese factories work on this basis (known as Just-in-Time techniques). Their philosophy is that stock of any kind is a bad thing, not only because of the costs of holding it, but also because stockholding is a way of covering up inefficiencies in procurement, production and marketing. By creating close relationships with a small number of suppliers, preferably near their premises, and placing long-term contracts, lead times can be reduced by having regular reliable deliveries, so keeping stock to a minimum.

Could you reduce your stocks? Controlling stock levels depends on three factors: accurate forecasting of sales; reliable and up-to-date stock and production records; organized purchasing supported by efficient suppliers.

If you hold stock, whether it be *raw materials* for making into products; *work in progress*; or *finished goods* for selling on to the customer, you should already have some sort of physical stock recording system in operation and no doubt your accountant has helped you arrive at a method of valuing stock. Do you also know how long different categories of stock have been held for? This needs to be monitored regularly (see Figure 5) since the longer the stock is held, the greater the stockholding cost is likely to be, including storage and insurance.

Figure 5   Stock ageing analysis

Stock category

	Age of stock in months						
	under 1	1–2	2–3	3–6	6–12	over 12	Total
	£	£	£	£	£	£	£
Raw materials							
Components							
Work in progress							
Finished stock							
TOTALS							

At least annually it is worth reviewing actual usage of slow-moving stock items and the potential usage over the next 12 months. This is necessary to determine not only the proper value of such stock for balance sheet purposes but also to determine if it is worth retaining. The answer may well be to decide to dispose of some slow-moving items at cost or below or even at scrap value where a market cannot be foreseen.

Find out your overall stock turnaround times with the following calculation:

$$\text{Number of times stock turned over} = \frac{\text{Cost of sales for the year}}{\text{Average value of stock}}$$

It's important here to use *cost* of sales for the year, rather than the actual sales values, since you need to compare like with like, ie cost of stock and cost of sales.

If, over the years, stock has grown faster than the increase in sales you are probably overstocked. You need to discover now precisely which stock items are making you money and which are slow-moving or redundant, so do the same calculation for raw materials and work in progress (substitute raw materials consumed for the cost of sales here); finished products and bought out goods for resale (if applicable); and for the different types of stock within each category.

Instead of expressing stock in terms of turnover, it can also be expressed in time:

$$\text{Number of days of stock} = \frac{\text{Value of stock}}{\text{Average daily cost of sales}}$$

This ratio warns you of slow-moving stocks as well as giving some guidance on how many days stock should be kept in hand.

This, admittedly rather tedious, exercise is worth the trouble since it alerts you to which are your fastest-moving items (and stock control should be tighter on these) and highlights old and redundant stock which you might want to sell off at reduced prices to release some money for the business. The traditional rule of thumb is that 80 per cent of your stock value will be held in 20 per cent of the items. Make sure you know which are your '20 per cent' and control them relentlessly.

If you find your stock is getting out of control, you need next to decide on the optimum stock level for each item, and the amount of stock to re-order and when.

Stock control systems are many and various, and it's an area where even simple computer systems can be a real help. Different types of stock need different systems of control too – one very simple system for small, low-value items is the 'Two Bin' system. Stock is kept in two bins. When the first bin is emptied, a withdrawal from the second bin triggers a re-order. The level of stock in the second bin will obviously be determined by anticipated order and delivery times.

More sophisticated methods are necessary for high-value items of stock. Here it is sensible to calculate the most economic ordering level by equating the cost of holding the stock with the cost of acquiring it. It may also be necessary to forecast possible price increases and any potential advantage of ordering ahead of such a possibility. Remember, you are investing precious liquid resources in stock and you need to be satisfied you are fully justified in doing so, in terms of optimum purchasing from suppliers and achieving the quality of service to customers which you require for success.

The question of *when* to order is dependent upon the lead time, which is the time interval between placing an order and receiving delivery, and stock usage during lead times. Lead time multiplied by the daily usage gives the minimum level of stock which should be held, and is commonly called the order point.

In real life, of course, businesses can't accurately anticipate demand, and deliveries don't always arrive when they are due. It is thus sensible to have some 'safety' stock – how much hinges on your forecasts of demand.

It is also worthwhile to seek alternative suppliers in terms of price, delivery and quality. With the developing impetus of the Single Market, and anticipated improvement in the speed of movement of goods, opportunities to purchase from European suppliers may become more viable.

Stock control courses

If the above exercises suggest that your stock could be better controlled and you would like to learn more about the procedures by which to do it, why not go on a short course? Several organizations run courses lasting two, three or five days. The courses run by the following bodies have all been rated 'good' by the National Training Index, an independent body which collects information on virtually every training course in the country and assesses them for the benefit of its members: Aldwark Management Training Ltd; CMTC Management Centre; Cranfield Institute of Technology; Institute of Purchasing and Supply; MSS Services Ltd; Purchasing Management Services (all addresses and telephone numbers in Appendix A).

Plugging money leaks

Your staff are often prime culprits when it comes to draining away your precious profits. For some strange reason, people who are perfectly upright and honest in every other way have an ambivalent attitude when it comes to 'taking' from their employer.

A survey carried out by Gallup in 1990 showed that only eight per cent of employees questioned regarded theft from the workplace as a crime worth reporting – if they saw a colleague stealing company property the rest said they would either ignore it or try to persuade the person not to do it, rather than report it to a superior.

Staff theft, admittedly, is mainly petty pilfering – but it all adds up. These are the main areas to watch for:

Expenses

Ways to fiddle them are legion – wining and dining friends on the company account; taking taxis where adequate public transport is available; claiming petrol for private car journeys and so on. It really is amazing how many large, and seemingly well-run, companies never question their employees' expense slips.

If you're running a tight ship you can't afford *not* to keep a close eye on what's being spent in your company's name. You should institute a clear policy on company expenses and tell staff at the outset what you consider to be genuine charges to the company. When, for instance, taxis can be used instead of trains and buses; what meals you are prepared to pay for if staff are away overnight; the rates you pay for petrol if they use their own car on company business; when it is legitimate to invite company contacts out for a meal – and what size bill you expect to see.

Expense slips should always be signed by the boss or a senior manager, and whoever has this task should take the time to vet them thoroughly, and ask questions where there is any room for doubt. The fact that employees know their expenses are going to be the subject of close scrutiny should deter would-be freeloaders.

Telephone calls

Chatting away for hours to friends and relations on the office phone is not only an abuse of the company's cash but a waste of the employee's time which the company is paying for. And time equals money.

It's a rather Draconian measure, though, to forbid staff to use the phone for private calls completely – people often need to sort out problems with organizations that can't be contacted out of office hours, or make last minute arrangements for collecting kids etc – but many firms do do it.

Better to tell staff that personal calls are discouraged, and allowable only if they're really important and outside Peak Rate telephone charges. If you don't think you can trust them, install a payphone for personal calls, or, if you want to be more flexible, monitor calls by investing in a call-logging system.

Call-loggers collect information such as where calls are made to (and which phone/extension made them), how long they last, and how much they cost. This information is presented in the form of a printed report which you then need to study and action.

Apart from allowing you to scrutinize what your staff are up to telephone-wise, call-logging systems allow you to see where savings can be made on genuine business calls; they are also a way of cross-checking your telephone bill.

It would be a mistake, though, to think that British Telecom will instantly accept that they have made an error, or dutifully refund the difference on an already-paid bill. BT will always credit the accuracy of their own meters above that of your call-logger but they should be more prepared to investigate discrepancies.

There is now an enormous range of call-logging systems available. The most basic, and the most common, are machines specifically designed to monitor phone traffic; then there are systems which form part of a multi-purpose computer, fitted with specially written call-logging software. These can provide very detailed information.

Some systems let you monitor separately calls to particular destinations or 'select' numbers so that you can see the amount of phone time spent talking to a particular person – very useful for businesses like solicitors and public relations firms which charge calls to their clients' accounts.

When questioned, firms which have installed call-logging systems seem to be satisfied that they have saved them money. One public relations firm said its system had paid for itself in two years, but warned that it did have to spend quite a lot of time wading through the print-outs to see who was making the most expensive calls.

The very existence of a call-logging system – make sure your staff know you have one – could well be enough of a deterrent where personal calls are concerned, but if you act on all the information it provides, you could genuinely keep your telephone costs down.

Fax messages

Fax machines are a new area to watch where staff are concerned – a director arriving at work before his secretary discovered a four-page 'love letter' from her boyfriend in New York, and subsequent enquiry elicited the information that this was a daily occurrence back and forth across the ocean! Faxing isn't cheap when you take into account the paper, electricity, machine lease charge and staff input time as well as the telephone charges. What's more, personal faxes tie up the machine and prevent urgent messages getting through.

Stationery cupboard

It can be a veritable goldmine for stocking up the home with a supply of envelopes, pens and paper. Keep it locked, and preferably only opened in the presence of a responsible member of staff who watches closely what's going where.

How to decide whether you can afford a new capital investment

Committing a lump sum for purchasing a new piece of machinery, a vehicle, or any capital investment eats into your funds and leaves you less money for the day-to-day running of the business. It is thus a big decision to make, and one where it is worth the time and trouble of calculating whether the net additional income from the asset will justify the cost.

If you're proposing to replace a machine, it's normal to calculate whether the new machine will produce cost savings. However, the cost savings alone may not cover the cost of the machine plus interest on the capital expended, and you will need to bring into the calculation any additional income it is likely to produce by increased output. For instance, the new machine may be faster and less prone to breakdown. Replacement of a machine which is working satisfactorily may be justified if there is a more efficient model on the market.

In making a replacement decision the saleable scrap value of the old equipment should be taken into account but its book value, after depreciation, is irrelevant. Any loss or profit on the book value compared with the sales value is the result of past surpluses or deficiencies of depreciation, and the past is dead as far as the accountants are concerned.

If you delay replacement until a machine or a vehicle is continually breaking down, with consequent loss of production and sales, replacement becomes inevitable and there's little point in making any calculations at all, except to choose the most suitable replacement. Here, you might ask yourself why you didn't make the decision earlier.

Some investments, of course, are unquantifiable and depend entirely on the vision and experience of managers. These might include projects for enhancing the company image, such as commissioning the design of a new company logo, or doing something to improve staff amenities.

If, however, you want to acquire additional assets for operational purposes, it's essential to make careful estimates of the additional income and the additional outgoings likely to arise from the investment.

Present value

There are several ways to do this, but the most satisfactory is to assess the additional cash flow likely to be produced by the asset. However, a straightforward projection of cash flows over the next few years won't tell you the whole truth – £100 in 1991 won't be worth £100 in 1996, so you need to discount the cash flows to arrive at a figure known as 'present value'.

Discounting cash flow simply means calculating the amount you would accept *now* for a payment, or series of payments, due in the future at a given rate of interest, eg if £110 was due to you in a year's time and you could earn ten per cent on your money, you would accept a payment of £100 now because you could invest that amount to produce £110 in a year. You have discounted the £110 to its present value.

Present value is arrived at by multiplying the net cash flow by the discount factor. You don't need to work out the discount figure yourself, though, discount tables are published in various books and stored in many financial calculators.

By working out the net cash flow (estimated revenue less estimated costs) of a given investment over a period of years, discounting those cash flows to their present value and deducting the initial investment, you can quickly see whether the investment makes financial sense. If the present value is a positive figure, it does; if negative, it doesn't.

By carrying out the same calculation on several different possible investments, you can then compare the present value of each and see immediately which is best in terms of a real return on your money. Case Story 2 shows how it works in practice.

Case Story 2

How discounted cash flow works in practice

The managing director of a printing works had to decide whether to invest £27,000 in a new machine. He would have to borrow the £27,000 from the bank so it was not a decision he – or the bank – could take lightly.

He also had to decide whether it would be a better investment to acquire a two-colour printing machine to enable him to expand his printing capacity or a stitching and gathering machine to save sub-contracting this operation.

For the purposes of the calculation he assumed both machines would have a useful life of five years with no scrap value. He forecast that the two-colour machine would produce the following additional revenue and costs (including over-heads and interest):

Year	Revenue £	Costs £	Net Cash Flows £
1	+50000	−45000	+ 5000
2	+80000	−70000	+10000
3	+80000	−70000	+10000
4	+80000	−70000	+10000
5	+50000	−45000	+ 5000
			+40000

He knew that if he invested £27,000 in a building society he could earn interest at ten per cent per annum compounded over the five years. By reversing the compound principle and applying it to the net cash flows with discount factors he restated the flows in present day terms. Here are the figures:

Year	Net Cash Flows £	Discount Factor	Present Value £
0	−27000		−27000
1	+ 5000	0.9091	+ 4545
2	+10000	0.8264	+ 8264
3	+10000	0.7213	+ 7513
4	+10000	0.6830	+ 6830
5	+ 5000	0.6209	+ 3105
		Net Present Value	+ 3257

The positive net present value of £3,257 meant the project was a worthwhile investment (assuming that the MD had got his estimates of future revenue and costs approximately right). In fact, any positive NPV would have suggested the same. A negative figure, however, would have shown that from a purely financial point of view, the MD would have been better off putting his money in the building society with a ten per cent return.

So what about the stitching and gathering machine? The investment was the same but the MD estimated that the net cash flows over five years would amount to slightly more − £40,500 as against £40,000. However, there was a considerable difference between the cash flows in each year, with much more coming in during Year 5. Here are the figures:

Year	Revenue £	Costs £	Net Cash Flows £
1	+ 10000	− 7000	+ 3000
2	+ 10000	− 7000	+ 3000
3	+ 15000	−11000	+ 4000
4	+ 50000	−40000	+10000
5	+100500	−80000	+20500
			+40500

Year	Net Cash Flows £	Discount Factor £	Present Value £
0	−27000		−27000
1	+ 3000	0.9091	+ 2727
2	+ 3000	0.8264	+ 2479
3	+ 4000	0.7513	+ 3005
4	+10000	0.6830	+ 6830
5	+20500	0.6209	+12728
		Net Present Value	+ 769

What the NPVs demonstrate is that the second machine, in spite of producing higher cash flows over the five years, is a much poorer investment than the first. Remember, it's not simply the net cash flows that are important but *when* they arise.

If the decision you need to make is whether or not to replace one asset with another, the factors you need to consider are: the present saleable value of the existing asset; the cost, including installation, of the replacement asset; the residual value of the replacement asset at the end of the term of years selected for the exercise; the estimated future annual operating costs of a) the existing asset and b) the replacement asset; the productivity of the replacement asset compared with the old asset, eg relative operating speeds of machines, capacity of vans etc. Various other factors may be relevant in particular cases – taxation effects and unquantifiable aspects such as customer reactions and staff safety.

The rate of interest you use for discounting the cash flows is called the 'cost of capital'. For practical purposes the rate should be the higher of a) the return you would get by further investment in the business and b) the borrowing rate for the business if it relied on a loan. Figure 6 shows a worked example for a firm trying to decide whether it makes sense to purchase a new van.

Figure 6   Replacement of a van

A retailing firm wants to know whether to replace its existing delivery van with a new one, or to hang on to the old one for a bit longer.

The existing van has a saleable value of £4,000; estimated operating costs for the next three years are: £3,000, £3,500 and £4,000; estimated residual value at the end of three years is nil. (The original cost and accumulated depreciation are irrelevant for this exercise.)

The replacement van would cost £11,000; estimated residual value after three years: £5,000; estimated operating costs for the next three years: £2,000, £2,000, £2,300.

This is the first set of figures:

COMPARATIVE CASH FLOWS (cash outflow in brackets)

Years	0	1	2	3	Total
(a) Retain existing van:					
operating costs		(3,000)	(3,500)	(4,000)	(10,500)
(b) Replace with new van:					
cost of new van	(11,000)				(11,000)
sale of old van	4,000				4,000
residual value of new van				5,000	5,000
operating costs		(2,000)	(2,000)	(2,300)	(6,300)
	(7,000)	(2,000)	(2,000)	2,700	(8,300)

Difference on replacement:

additional outflow	7,000				
reduced outflow		1,000	1,500	6,700	2,200

Now the difference on replacement figures has to be discounted at an appropriate rate of interest to show what the putative future saving of £2,200 will really be in terms of present value.

The retailer decides to discount the investment by a) 15 per cent being the interest it would pay to borrow the money to buy the van, and, b) 10 per cent interest which is what the firm believes it could earn on its capital if it didn't borrow.

Discounting at 15%

Year	Actual cash flows	Discount factor	Present values
0	£(7,000)		(7,000.0)
1	1,000	0.8696	869.6
2	1,500	0.7561	1,134.2
3	6,700	0.6575	4,405.2
	£2,200		£(591.0)

Discounting at 10%

0	£(7,000)		(7,000.0)
1	1,000	0.9091	909.1
2	1,500	0.8264	1,239.6
3	6,700	0.7513	5,033.7
	£2,200		£182.4

These calculations show that purchasing a new van is not a good idea if the money has to be borrowed, but could be marginally beneficial if the company already has the money and can really earn ten per cent on its capital.

3

Could you be more profitable?

Cutting costs, the subject of the last chapter, is, of course, one of the ways to maximize profitability, and one which has a relatively fast impact on cash flow. Other ways to boost profits are by raising prices and by selling more of your existing products/service (or, more long-term, developing additional products to sell to existing and new customers). These are less easy methods to control, though, since they are affected by what's happening in your marketplace. In addition, their impact on cash flow may take time to show results.

Raising prices is a gamble that might rebound on you too: if the market won't stand the rise, sales might drop to a level that means your profit is lower than before. It thus needs careful consideration of competitive pricing policies and shrewd judgment about how your product, its delivery and after sales service compares with competitors.

Selling more will certainly increase profit – but watch out for the effect it's likely to have on your cash flow. More sales usually mean more expenditure in terms of stock, materials and marketing, and suppliers need paying long before you can expect to get paid for the extra sales.

Paying your creditors is the other side of the cash flow equation from extracting money from your debtors and part of the delicate balancing act involved in controlling working capital, so it's just as important to formulate a policy for payments out as it is for cash collection.

Once money is received it needs to be put to work for your business as quickly as possible, so advice on getting cheques cleared faster is included in this chapter. So too is information on how to cover yourself against potential bad debts with credit insurance – it might seem an obvious way to offset the risk, but it's pretty pricey.

Rationalizing business activities

Businesses need to be lean and mean to survive in these competitive times. Every member of staff, every inch of space and every machine and system should be utilized to full capacity.

If you are a manufacturing business and find you have spare capacity, consider touting around for subcontracted orders from other firms. Provided you cover your additional materials, labour and running costs, any additional income will effectively be cash profit to the business. Or, consider whether it wouldn't be cheaper to subcontract some of your own operations, thus freeing any working capital tied up in the process and letting someone else risk their money.

Sometimes it makes sense to stay out of production altogether. One new firm, launching a product deliberately designed so that the final 'manufacturing operation' was simply an assembly and packing task which the firm intended to do itself, found that it could make colossal savings by subcontracting the work.

Outside manufacturing firms, anxious to make use of spare capacity, were quoting 80p per unit compared with the firm's own costing of £3.20 per unit. Putting the work out also enabled this firm to concentrate on the things it was best at – product design and marketing.

Chambers of Commerce, Enterprise Agencies and trade associations can often help match manufacturers with subcontractors, and trade magazines carry ads for this sort of thing. The Engineering Industries Association (see Appendix A) operates a 'capacity exchange service' through its regional offices. An exhibition, SUBCON, completely devoted to subcontracting is held at the National Exhibition Centre, Birmingham every two years (next one May 1992).

Concentrate your energies and cash on the product and service lines that actually make you money. There is a piece of business lore called the Pareto Principle or the 80/20 rule which says that 80 per cent of the effort goes into producing 20 per cent of the results. So be brutal about discarding those lines which are not bringing in adequate profit, unless, of course, they are vital to complete the range of products which your major customers expect to buy from you.

Premises and people

If you occupy more space than you need, consider rationalizing the way you use your accommodation to make a self-contained section to let off to someone else for work space or for storage (presuming your lease allows you to do this). Alternatively, consider using the spare space to diversify into other related activities if you have the working capital to do so or can borrow it without undermining your core activity.

Too many stockrooms/ warehouses are crammed full of slow-moving lines. Review your stock situation (see previous chapter) and consider having a sale to turn old and slow-moving stock into valuable cash.

Getting rid of people who aren't fully pulling their weight is a difficult and emotive thing to do, but you can't afford to carry dead wood. Could you allocate other responsibilities to those who don't have enough to do? If debt-collecting is your major problem, you could probably train up underworked sales or accounts staff to carry out this job supported by a sales bonus scheme based on collections, and not sales.

If letting staff go is the only answer, do it quickly, and, once done, put it behind you and cut short staff post-mortems on what went wrong. The chances are your star performers will understand anyhow – they may well have resented the fact that you were carrying people who were underperforming – and will feel more positive as a result, particularly if you take the time to speak to each one individually.

If finding enough time to do all the necessary tasks is the main problem your business faces, consider employing outside specialists to take some of the load off your back. These could be, for instance, mailing houses to look after any bulk mailings you plan to customers; debt collection agencies to help improve your credit control; corporate hospitality firms to organize staff or client outings; typing agencies etc. Weigh up their charges against the time it would take to do the work in-house, given that specialists will probably do it quicker (and probably better), plus the time it releases to do other important things.

Consultants

If it's *your* time as a manager which is in short supply, consider calling in consultants to take over those tasks you are least good at. Consultants are widely viewed as a big company extravagance, out of reach of smaller outfits, yet an able consultant can be a particularly cost-effective solution for managers of small businesses, too beset with day-to-day affairs to find the time to assess and implement new initiatives, or too close to a particular problem to see the solution clearly. And it's cheaper than taking on an employee since you don't carry any of the consultant's overheads – he carries out a specific task for an agreed fee. If he's successful you should more than recoup his costs.

The Government is currently offering help with consultancy costs to firms employing fewer than 500 people through its Enterprise Initiative scheme. Until 1994, the Government is offering to pay half the cost (two-thirds in areas designated Urban Programme Areas) of between five and 15 days of consultancy on the following topics: *marketing*, *quality control*, *design*, *manufacturing systems*, *business planning*, *financial and information systems*, *exporting*. Interested firms should contact their local Department of Trade and Industry office (see Appendix A) for more details. Most of the firms taking advantage of the Enterprise Initiative to date had never used consultants before and, interestingly, two out of three businesses completing consultancy projects saw an increase in profits in the first year.

The organizers of the various Enterprise Initiatives maintain lists of approved consultants. If you don't wish to take advantage of the EI but need a consultant, bear in mind that there are consultants and consultants. If possible, get a recommendation from a business colleague, or play safe by contacting the relevant professional body for the names of suitable consultants. The Management Consultants Association can help you find a management consultant; the Chartered Institute of Marketing, a marketing consultant; the Association of Professional Computer Consultants a computer consultant (see Appendix A for addresses). For other more specialized types of consultancy help contact the relevant professional body which you will find listed in either the *Directory of British Associations* or *Councils, Committees and Boards*, available in most good reference libraries.

Student power

If your firm is hard pressed for money and manpower, free or inexpensive help is often available from the academic world. Many business students need part-time experience in a real-life business environment, and redundant executives, equipped with an array of skills and qualifications, are being recycled into the system by universities and polytechnic business schools. Students at art colleges, too, will often jump at the opportunity to cut their teeth designing a company's brochures or promotional material.

Students aren't the only commodity the institutions can provide. Many universities and polytechnics offer advice and consultancy services to businesses, and some will make available their product-testing and other sophisticated facilities (usually for a fee). It's certainly worth putting out feelers to see what help of this kind is available in your area.

Two slightly more specialized student services are offered by the Brain Exchange and Scanmark (addresses in Appendix A). These cost – but less than you would pay for equivalent commercial services.

The Brain Exchange, run by AIESEC Great Britain Ltd provides overseas business students to work on projects for between eight weeks and 18 months. Scanmark, run by Buckingham College of Higher Education, will allocate a postgraduate student in the final year of an export marketing course to undertake market research in any part of the world.

The right price to charge

Although prices are really in the end determined by what customers will pay and what the competition charges, you need to monitor constantly the profit each of your products/services is making for you against the costs of producing/providing it. If it decreases, this inevitably affects your cash flow and you need to consider what to do.

Pricing is a very complex subject since costs, sales volume, selling price and profit are all inextricably linked. When costs go up, prices should follow suit, but since this is likely to reduce sales volume, a balancing act is involved to ensure you don't end up worse off. At the end of the day you are constrained by what the market will bear.

There is a handy equation which enables you to calculate some of the factors involved in pricing. If, for instance, you want to calculate the break-even point of the number of unit sales you would have to make at a given price just to cover costs, this is the calculation:

$$\text{Break even point} = \frac{\text{Fixed costs}}{\text{Unit selling price} - \text{variable costs per unit}}$$

Fixed costs are those overheads like rent and rates, administrative staff, light and heat, insurance, building maintenance and depreciation which do not move significantly with the level of production. Variable costs on the other hand move almost directly in relation to the level of production, and comprise materials, direct labour and running costs including plant maintenance and power.

Worked out, assuming fixed costs of £10,000, a selling price of £5 per unit and the variable cost per unit of £3, it looks like this:

$$\text{BEP} = \frac{£10,000}{£5 - £3} = \frac{£10,000}{£2} = 5,000 \text{ units}$$

So 5,000 units need to be sold at £5 each before you would show any profit. If you know the profit you would like to achieve you can add it into the equation thus:

$$\text{Break even profit point} = \frac{\text{Fixed costs} + \text{desired profits}}{\text{Unit selling price} - \text{variable unit costs}}$$

Say your desired profit was £10,000:

$$\text{BEPP} + \frac{£10,000 + £10,000}{£5 - £3} = \frac{£20,000}{£2} = 10,000 \text{ units}$$

Maybe it isn't possible to sell or produce that volume. If so, something has to alter – costs reduced or a higher selling price.

If you know the maximum number of units it is practicable to sell or produce, you can work out the break even profit price by turning the sales volume/price equation round. Say it's 7,000:

$$7,000 = \frac{£10,000 + £10,000}{£x - £3} = £5.86$$

This means that given the maximum capacity and the profit objective, the price will be £5.86. If the market will stand that price, well and good. If not, ways will have to be found to decrease costs or find additional customers. Alternatively, a lower profit will have to be accepted. The joy of this equation is that it allows you to calculate each element until you reach a satisfactory conclusion.

Knowing your break-even profit point also allows you to see by how much you could afford to lower prices to achieve more sales quickly if you need to free up funds. Bear in mind when considering pricing that it isn't always necessary to sell the same product at the same price to all customers. One firm which sells its product to both the public sector and to domestic consumers finds maximum profitability by pricing up to the former and down to the latter. As these customers have no dealings with each other, the firm gets the best of both worlds.

Ways to stimulate sales

Boosting your sales obviously increases the amount of cash coming into your business, but your very survival depends on your ability to market and sell your products effectively. Even if sales appear to be growing steadily each year and you are showing profit, your market might still be slipping away from you without you being aware of it.

Do you, for instance, take into account inflation when analysing your sales figures? Converting pounds for previous years into current pounds by applying the Retail Price Index figure for the current year and dividing it by the Index figure for the year in question often produces a quite different picture of growth. Competitors too might be quietly eroding your share of the market and all products have a natural life cycle anyhow (although this can often be extended by continuing product innovation). Thus, there should be no let-up in your marketing activity and it should be properly planned and budgeted for each year.

Presuming you have got the basics right, ie you are selling the right product/service at the right price to the right people, ask yourself these questions: is enough time being devoted to marketing and selling? Smaller businesses where the owners wear many hats, often find they get so bogged down in detail that they neglect this vital function. Look at your product and sales literature – is it informative and inviting? Would it make you want to buy?

Do you stress the benefits, rather than the features, of what you're selling in your advertising and sales patter? Many advertisers confine themselves to a description of what's on offer, or worse, merely sing their own praises – 'We've been established since 1890', 'We have 5,000 satisfied customers'. Prospective purchasers are only interested in what's in it for them if they buy the product, so the features of what you're selling need translating into benefits. A car, for example, might have these features: a five-speed gear box, a hatchback, rustproofing. The respective benefits are: *fuel economy when cruising, easy access to luggage space, keeps its looks and saves on respraying.*

There's no room to spell out all the secrets of successful marketing and selling in this chapter – dozens of good books are devoted to this subject alone. Here, though, are a few practical do's and don't's designed to help you stimulate sales:

- **Don't try to do too many things at once as many smaller firms do.** Remember the 80/20 rule, which, translated into selling terms, states that 80 per cent of profit comes from 20 per cent of sales effort or 20 per cent of products. See if this is true for your business and, if so, concentrate your energies and cash on that important 20 per cent and consider discarding products etc which are less profitable and not vital to your core business.
- **Don't automatically prune your promotional budget when times are bad.** Evidence suggests that firms which maintain, or even increase, promotional expenditure during a recession win out over meaner competitors. Cadbury's, for instance, promoted heavily during World War II when supplies were virtually non-existent – and reaped the benefits after the war.
- **Do bear in mind that existing customers are more valuable than new customers.** It is estimated that they are ten to 25

times more likely to buy from you than cold prospects. Money spent promoting to them is therefore more likely to give you a better return on your investment.

Here are a few simple ways to encourage repeat business: if you sell expendable supplies such as stationery, health products, flower seeds, enclose a blank order form, completed, if possible, so that the customer only has to sign it. If you sell other manufacturers' equipment, append your own nameplate or sticker with the words 'For sales, service and sundries contact . . .'

If you're selling an expensive product or service, consider telephoning the purchaser a few days after the sale to thank him or her and enquire whether everything is satisfactory. Customers are known to warm to suppliers who extend this small courtesy. What's more, they're likely to tell their friends. If the order is posted, enclose a letter thanking the customer for the purchase and drawing attention to other items which you think might be of interest. If the item can be described as 'new' or 'just released' the results will be even better.

- **Do look for neat little ways to get the edge over your competitors**. A garage owner, for instance, noticed that his main competitor had stopped valeting customers' cars when they came in for service – as an economy measure. This garage owner promptly introduced car and engine cleaning as standard with every service, and dramatically increased his clientele.

- **Do consider using some of the wheezes which have worked for others in pushing up sales**. Here are a few examples which can be adapted to different types of business:

  - *Get-a-friend offers*. Contact your list of satisfied customers and offer them a free gift for providing the names and addresses of three or four friends who might also appreciate your product or service. Offer a more substantial gift if any of the friends turn into customers.

  - *The one-penny sale, or two for the price of one*. Offer selected products at normal prices but, for a limited period, tell customers that if they take two, they get the second one for a penny, or for no extra charge. This technique has more publicity value than a normal sale which often smacks of a clear-out anyhow.

- *The millionth customer.* Put up a prominent notice saying 'Some time during the next 30 days we will be welcoming our one millionth customer. He or she will receive their entire purchase FREE with the compliments of the management. Will you be the lucky person?' Since the winner isn't told the good news until after making the purchase, this encourages everyone to spend more than normal. It doesn't, of course, need to be the millionth customer – it could be the hundredth, thousandth, five thousandth and so on.

- *The incomplete gift.* Prospects are mailed half a gift or something that only works with something else. An electronics firm, for example, mailed earphones for a personal stereo to its prime prospects, telling them that they could collect the stereo itself if they called at the firm's exhibition stand. Needless to say, the stand in question overflowed all day.

- **Do ensure that you are getting the best from your salespeople.** Very often the only two things a company monitors are expenses and orders but these don't reveal whether salespeople are really making the best use of their (your) time – ie the time spent effectively in front of target customers (Case Story 4 shows what a shock lay in store for one MD when he followed his salespeople around with a stopwatch).

    Analyse the ratio of total calls to: first ever calls/quotation requests/demonstrations/quotation follow-ups/orders taken or promised/new accounts opened/complaints and service calls/ miles per call. Keeping an eye on these ratios for each salesperson will show, over a period, where the weaknesses lie.

Case Story 3

Selling tip

Here's a zany selling idea used with great success by an American insurance salesman. He has to cross a toll bridge every day on his way to work. He always trys to get in just ahead of a Rolls Royce or some other expensive car. When he hands the money over to the cashier he says, 'I'm paying for

---

> my car and the one behind as well. Just give him my card when he goes through'. On the card he writes 'With compliments, Bill Jones'. He claims it sells him millions of dollars worth of life insurance every year.

- **Do set targets for your salespeople and consider how to reward those who meet/exceed their targets**. Some firms reward by commission, some by gifts/incentive travel, while others believe that good salaries and good training are the best motivators. One sly manager faced with the problem of re-motivating a salesman who had done so well he was beginning to rest on his laurels, invented a fictitious super-salesman who, he claimed, had worked for the company many years before. This super-salesman, said the manager, had once made ten sales in a row, a record nobody else had been able to match. It worked. The lethargic salesman took the bait and worked like stink until at last he hit the target, and, such was his enthusiasm, he made sales on his next two calls as well!
- **Do give some thought to whether telephone selling could be substituted for face-to-face selling**. It will save you a great deal of money in costs per contact and also enable far more prospects to be contacted each day. However, it is not right for every business and some customers bitterly resent being contacted by telephone. Test it first.

  One firm discovered by accident that sales actually rocketed when the salesman was *only* able to contact customers by phone for six months because he was laid up with a broken leg. Admittedly, he got a fair bit of sympathy business initially, but the boom continued and the real reason, he decided, was that he was able to contact customers far more often than when he was visiting them personally, and *his* particular customers were quite happy buying over the phone.
- **Do consider using your engineers as salespeople**. If you're a business selling goods which need service or repair, teach your engineers to keep their eyes and ears open for potential new business. Engineers generally get to see customers more frequently than do salespeople. What's more customers trust them better. This opportunity to build up good relationships can pay dividends when it comes to decisions on improving or

replacing existing equipment since in today's competitive conditions, the deciding factor more often than not is the quality of the back-up service provided.

Engineers need to be every bit as responsive to customers as salespeople. Companies tend to look on them as people who can offer impartial advice, and managers frequently consult them for information on the costs or advisability of replacing or adding to existing equipment. Engineers should be instructed to let the managers do most of the talking but make mental notes, and write down the gist of the discussion when they are on their own and then pass the information to the people in the company who can turn that information into a sale.

It does work. One service engineer helped his firm land a three-quarter million contract for computer equipment just by reporting a conversation he heard in the firm's canteen to his boss. If your engineers are motivated and primed to be constantly on the alert wherever they go they may also spot selling opportunities further afield. Another engineer was responsible for an order worth £1.7 million. He noticed that an office block next to a client he regularly attended had been taken by a new electronics firm which was a prime prospect for his firm's test equipment. He reported back, the salespeople went in and secured the order.

Case Story 4

Monitoring sales performance

The MD of a contract furnishing company was concerned that he wasn't getting the best out of his salesforce. He decided to spend a few days surreptitiously monitoring their performance with the aid of a stopwatch. First, he monitored how they spent their time.

He discovered that his best salesman spent, on average, 70 per cent more time in front of customers than the worst salesman. The best salesman didn't work any longer hours, he just worked smarter. The best salesman had a detailed plan of his territory with his potential customers plotted on a map. He used a systematic method of covering the ground to make sure

---

his time was spent effectively. The worst salesman had no overall plan. He responded to the latest lead, phone call or problem, zig-zagging back and forth across his territory. He justified this as 'retaining maximum flexibility'.

When it came to measuring the average call rate and the effectiveness of the calls, the results were as follows:

Analysis	Worst Salesman	Best Salesman	% Difference
Calls made	3	5	+67
Effective calls made	2	5	+150
Average contact time	50 mins	34 mins	−37
Average effective contact time	16 mins	26 mins	+62.5

The worst salesman made, on average, only three calls per day and one of these was largely useless since the person was a 'suspect' rather than a 'prospect' — ie he had no current need of the company's products. Bad luck you might say, but bad planning is the more likely explanation.

The best salesman made, on average, five calls a day and each was effective because he had done sufficient probing and background research before going in. What's more, each call took less time than those of his less efficient colleague. The 'worst' salesman spent 45 minutes in one call listening to his client talking about his holiday. When challenged by his MD he said 'It would have been rude to interrupt', and, in any case, he was 'building up a relationship with the client'. The real reason was simply that this call had no clear objectives and he had lost control of the interview.

When the MD analysed the results over a year, he found he was getting only 115 effective selling hours from his worst salesman — with the average salesman costing around £30,000 a year that works out at £260 per hour (based on 215 selling days per year), rather more than a first class QC! The best salesman was spending 466 hours selling each year — over four times the level of the worst. And it showed in results. The best salesman had more than double the annual sales rate and four times the new account opening rate of the worst salesman.

Paying your debts

Your trade creditors are a good source of short-term finance and it is inevitably much easier to delay payments to them than it is to extract money from customers. However, tempting though this is, taking a long time to pay your debts is a slippery slope which needs to be trodden very carefully – it can lead to a refusal to supply you in the future, higher prices and, of course, you risk getting dragged through the courts. Also, although delaying payment gives you additional working capital, this could turn sour if there is a downturn in business and you have to repay it out of a reduced cash flow.

As a rough rule of thumb you should be looking for as much credit from your suppliers as you are giving to your customers. Needless to say, this is not always easy to achieve. The following ratio gives you an idea of how many days on average you are taking to pay your creditors:

$$\text{Average credit period} = \frac{\text{Creditors}}{\text{Purchases}} \times 365$$

If, for instance, total purchases made in the year ending on the balance sheet date were £12 million and the payments outstanding in respect of these purchases at the balance sheet date were £2 million, then the average length of credit taken (£2 million/£12 million × 365) was 60 days or two months. Is this the same length of time your debtors are taking to pay you?

An 'aged creditor analysis' (see Figure 7) which shows how much is, and has been, owing for how long to which suppliers is one of the reports you need to prepare regularly if you are to keep close tabs on your financial position.

Figure 7 Aged creditors analysis

ACCOUNT	MONTHS OVERDUE			Actual overdue	Not yet due	Total
	3+	2	1			
	£	£	£	£	£	£
A						
B						
C						
D						
etc						
TOTALS						

Although many businesses operate a policy for getting cash in, far fewer exercise the same degree of control on payments out, but it is just as important when it comes to monitoring cash flow.

A simple system for smaller firms is to have an unpaid invoice file, a paid invoice file and a day book. All invoices are entered by date order in the day book and transferred from one file to the other once paid, with a note stating when payment was made written in the day book. This enables the manager to see at a glance how much is owed and to which suppliers.

Businesses with a more substantial number of transactions should keep a separate ledger in which details of purchases are entered in sequence by transaction, and there should be a Creditors' Ledger in which each supplier who gives credit has an individual account. When an order is placed, a copy should go straight to the accounts department. When the goods are received they should be examined immediately to see that they correspond with the order, and a note to that effect, or details of any damage or shortfall in quantity or quality, sent to the accounts department.

Invoices should go straight to the accounts department for initial recording and checking against the purchase order. Without this discipline invoices can languish in staff in-trays with the result that payments are delayed and relationships with suppliers become strained.

If there was no purchase order, the invoice should be sent to whoever placed the order to check and sign – again the accounts department should keep a record of when invoices were passed to whom in case the people concerned simply sit on them. If all is well, the invoice should be passed for payment and ideally paid at the expiry of the supplier's stated payment period.

Many firms keep their administration costs down by using a batch-payment system, ie just having one payment run each month. This is also an aid to forecasting cash flow, although exceptions might have to be made for invoices offering discounts for early settlement which will probably have to be processed in between payment runs.

These are the only invoices it is worth paying before the due date. A discount of, say, 2.5 per cent for payment within ten rather than 30 days is equivalent to an interest rate of 46 per cent which compares very favourably with the cost of borrowing money. In fact, it is often cheaper to increase the overdraft to meet such bills (Chapter 5 shows you how to work out the interest rate of a discount). Accounts staff should be instructed to bring any invoices offering discounts for early settlement to the attention of the management for a quick decision.

If it's a question of only being able to pay some but not all the debts due on a certain date, common sense suggests that the priorities should be to pay first those invoices offering early settlement discounts and vital suppliers where your business would be jeopardized if supplies were withdrawn. Human nature being what it is, the chances are that you'll pay next those people who hassle for payment hardest and leave till the last those who don't bother to chase their debts. Reverse the situation and you see the advantages of operating a proper credit control policy yourself.

Sometimes, of course, the money just isn't there to pay even the most important creditors on the due date. Where payment is delayed this should be a deliberate business policy and not just made at the whim of someone in the accounts department. If creditors can't be paid on time, it is politic to inform them and perhaps give them a date when payment can be expected, or even offer them staged payments.

VAT

You can't, though, afford to stall creditors like the Inland Revenue and Customs & Excise since they impose Draconian penalties for late payment. Accountants say that if you know you are going to have to default on your VAT payments, it's better simply to miss out one quarter completely rather than pay them all late. The first time you default you attract a five per cent penalty but higher penalties are levied for defaulting a second and subsequent times.

Its sensible, too, to delay sending out invoices near the end of a VAT quarter. If you do, you will have to pay the VAT on them within 30 days, whereas if you wait a few extra days, you get an extra three months' grace before the VAT is due.

Paying VAT the normal way, ie quarterly according to the invoices issued and received in the quarter, can be pretty bad news for firms with customers who take lengthy periods of credit since it's often necessary to pay the VAT before receiving the cash. If the annual value of your taxable supplies (excluding VAT) is not more than £300,000 you can apply to use the VAT Cash Accounting Scheme which allows you to account for VAT on the basis of the actual payments you receive and make, rather than on the invoice dates. This could make quite a difference to the cash flow of firms with many credit sales and not too many purchases. It also gives you automatic bad debt relief – if you are not paid by your customer, you don't have to account for VAT.

The Cash Accounting Scheme will be of no benefit to the cash flow of firms paid at the time the sale is made, or to firms where the amount of VAT reclaimed is more than the VAT paid in. Unfortunately, importers cannot use the Cash Accounting Scheme to account for VAT on the importation of goods or on their removal from a warehouse or a free zone. They can, though, use the scheme to account for VAT on the onward supply of these goods in the UK.

You might also find it less time-consuming to make one VAT return per year, instead of four. The VAT Annual Accounting Scheme allows you to do this but you have to make payments on account by direct debit throughout the year. Details of both these schemes are available from your local VAT office.

Employees

You can't delay payment to your employees but you can make more use of the money due to them by paying them monthly, rather than weekly, and payment by cheque, rather than cash, gives you a few extra days' credit. This, of course, won't apply if you pay by direct debit.

Case Story 5

Cash flow control kept tight and simple

CY, the director of a company with a £500,000 turnover, runs a very meticulous payment policy. He knows all too well the problems of not being able to meet his bills – his last company went into liquidation for just that reason and CY found it a very nasty experience.

Now he keeps payments totally under his own control and he monitors his cash flow every single week. On Sunday, CY works out exactly how much money he can expect in from debtors the following week. Based on that figure he then decides which of his creditors he will pay. He has two regular and essential suppliers and to these he pays a set amount each week rather than waiting for their monthly bill only to discover the money isn't available to cover it. Next he pays any small invoices (up to £150) 'just to get them out of the way'. Then he pays creditors according to the age of the invoice – and their value to his business. But, if during the week, the money expected in doesn't seem to be materializing, he holds fire until there is enough money there to cover the payments. Knowing he will have problems finding the money to pay the quarterly VAT bills, he advises the bank well in advance when these are coming in and arranges an extension of his overdraft to cover them.

CY used to get very annoyed when he dunned debtors for payment and they said: 'You'll be on the payment run in two weeks time'. Now he sees the value of using this ploy when creditors phone him. It means he has two weeks grace and can slot them into his payment programme for two weeks' time, and *they* know exactly when they will get their money.

Terms of payment

Do you know what your creditors' terms of payment mean? Here is an explanation of the most commonly used payment terms:

- **Nett monthly**: settlement for one month's deliveries or one month's invoices is due at (or before) the end of the following month.
- **Nett 30 days**: invoices should be settled within 30 days from the date of the invoice. The same principle applies to seven, 14, 21 or any other number of days.
- **Settlement by 21st of the following month**: the money is due by the 21st of the month following the date of the invoice.
- **Stage or progress payments**: this is usual where there is a long manufacturing or delivery period. It is common for a down payment to be made before the work commences with the balance payable at agreed stages of completion or manufacture.
- **Cash on delivery (COD)**: a cheque to be given to the delivery people.
- **Load over load**: payment for the previous delivery is made before the current delivery is handed over.

Getting cheques cleared faster

Payments received are no use as funds for your business until they have been credited to your account, and the time-lag between receiving payment and the date it actually has value can vary tremendously depending on your own procedures and where you and your respective payees keep their accounts – building societies, for instance, take ten days to process a cheque.

Cheques are the most common form of business payment – although you might want to insist on a banker's draft or a bank-to-bank transfer if you need a cast-iron guarantee that your debtor has the money. Bear in mind, though, that these will bump up your bank charges.

When payment by cheque is made through the banking system, the time factor for clearance depends on which of these situations apply:

- If both payer and payee hold accounts at the same bank and branch the transfer is made the same day.
- If both payer and payee hold accounts at the same bank but at different branches the transfer is made within the bank's internal system, normally within one or two days.
- Where payer and payee hold accounts at different banks, the clearing system comes into operation.

There are different clearing organizations for different types of payment but the big banks belong to all of them. If non-member banks and, eg building societies, want to process cheques these have to be cleared through the member-banks, hence the longer time taken.

The standard time for clearing cheques is three business days, ie if you deposit a cheque at the bank on a Friday, the funds will be available to you by the following Wednesday. There is an exception for the City of London where cheques of over £10,000 get same-day clearance under the 'Town Clearing System' which is different from the General Clearing System.

Clerical and other time can be saved dramatically if you use one of the automated banking systems, such as BACS. Money can be paid in or received without leaving the premises and without the need to raise any paperwork. You need an IBM-compatible PC with a minimum of 640K RAM and a high specification modem to take advantage of it.

What you can do to get things moving faster

- You can ask the bank for special same-day clearance. However, the fee for this is quite high so it is probably only worth it for substantial payments, and even then it would be sensible to calculate first whether the reduced interest payments on your overdraft for three days comes to more than the clearance fee.
- If a large company regularly pays you sizeable cheques, consider opening a bank account at the branch the cheques are drawn on to get same-day clearance.
- If your customers are mainly in the City of London and pay you cheques over £10,000, think about opening a Town Clearing Account within the square mile to get same-day clearance.

See also how you can eliminate any delays at your end:

- Make sure your debtor knows exactly who the cheque is to be made out to so that bank delays can be avoided. This is particularly important if you're requesting a bank-to-bank transfer where the paying bank needs the precise details of the payee's bank and branch.
- Consider using a motor-cycle courier to round up cheques waiting for you in the postroom of your debtors rather than risking delays with the mail.
- Ensure that once a cheque is received, your accounts staff check it immediately: is the date correct? Is the cheque made out to the right party? Do the words and figures agree? Is it signed? Check also that procedures are in place to get it into the bank as rapidly as possible.

Insuring against bad debts

Taking out insurance against non-payment by customers seems, on the face of it, the perfect solution to the bad debt problem. However, credit insurance is pretty expensive – usually somewhere between 0.25 and one per cent of turnover, so it's a decision that needs careful thought.

It's probably not worth insuring your credit if you have a large number of small accounts since bad debts on these are unlikely to send you to the wall, although, of course, they will have an adverse effect on profits. If, though, you have a few large accounts and the failure of a major client would be disastrous, then it's a sensible investment. There are special insurance schemes for companies that export (see Chapter 8).

You need to equate the cost of the insurance with the risks involved to decide whether the insurance is justified. The alternative is to accept the risk and create a provision for bad debts in your cash planning.

Credit insurance protects you against your customers' *insolvency* – it doesn't cover you against slow payers. It isn't always essential that firms be formally declared insolvent, but if they aren't the insurers will require evidence of 'protracted default' and inability to pay. The level of cover is normally between 75 and 90 per cent of the sale value, up to an agreed credit limit, and premiums vary according to the level of risk. Credit insurance

Figure 8 Proposal for credit insurance
This extract from an insurance company's application form shows that good credit management is a pre-requisite for taking out credit insurance

---

2. PRESENT CREDIT CONTROL PROCEDURE

(a) Are terms of payment shown   (Tick YES or NO box as appropriate)
   (i) on invoices?   Y☐   N☐
   (ii) on statements?   Y☐   N☐

(b) Are credit limits operated?   Y☐   N☐
   (i)   How are they recorded?

   (ii) Who sets the credit limits?

   (iii) Who decides on the terms of payment?

(c) Who authorises orders for credit?

(d) Is reference made to the state of the accounts
   (i)   When orders are received?   Y☐   N☐
   (ii) When orders are ready for delivery or the
        work is about to be done or the service
        rendered?   Y☐   N☐

(e) What action is taken if
   (i)   The limit would be exceeded by
        accepting the order?

   (ii) The account is overdue when an order is
        received?

(f) Is the credit control procedure known to other
departments?   Y☐   N☐

---

3. ACCOUNTING PROCEDURE

Is it Manual?_____ Mechanical?_____ Computerised?_____

When are invoices raised for goods delivered/
work done/service rendered?   Same day _____ Within _____ days

When are they posted to the ledger?   Same day _____ Within _____ days

How soon are they sent out?   Same day _____ Within _____ days

To what day each month are statements made up?

How many days after this date are they sent out   _____ No. of days

Is an age analysis produced?   Y☐   N☐

How frequently?   Every ____ days   Once a month ____

Do statements show age analysis?   Y☐   N☐

Reproduced by kind permission of Trade Indemnity PLC

premiums are a tax-allowable expense, though.

The type of cover you can buy varies. Some policies cover your whole customer list, others just particular customers, or all customers over a certain limit.

The forms you fill in when you apply for credit insurance ask searching questions about your individual customers and your own credit control procedures (see Figure 8) and, prior to granting a policy, the insurer is likely to insist on changes in your procedures if it's thought improvements are needed. The insurer will also lay down the steps you must take to check the credit-worthiness of your customers.

You shouldn't let any of this put you off – the insurer is actually doing you a favour by advising you how to smarten up your credit control and thus improve results.

The insurer will scrutinize your list of clients and suggested credit limits and decide whether to agree or reject particular customers and/or limits. Take heed if the insurer refuses to cover a company – insurers have alert eyes and ears in the marketplace and may know something you don't.

Once insured, you are required to report immediately when an account becomes overdue. If you learn, though, that a customer is in financial trouble before the money is due you should tell the insurers without delay. You are also required to make regular returns to the insurers so that they are aware of the risks they are carrying for you.

Factoring is another method of insuring against bad debts and it also frees the funds you have tied up in debtors which can then be used to finance growth (factoring is discussed at length in Chapter 9).

4

Can your customers pay their bills?

When you grant credit do you check up on potential customers before you offer it, or, like many firms, do you consider this unnecessary because you're only too grateful for any business that comes your way?

There are plenty of good reasons for not being too trusting. Bad debts can cancel out profit in one fell swoop, and debtors often represent the largest asset a business has. This combined with the fact that during 1990 business failures were running at a ten-year high suggests that it's crazy not to take some steps to discover whether your customers are likely to pay you or not.

Several different ways of determining credit-worthiness are explained below – the more checks you make, the safer your money is likely to be, and therefore your business.

Get your salespeople to discover

There's a quick and easy way to assess new customers for credit which many firms overlook: ask your salespeople to find out. Salespeople act anyhow as the eyes and ears for your business and the information they need to collect to get to know prospective customers well enough to sell to them can also be used to establish the customer's ability to pay debts.

This costs you nothing and gives you inside information from the best source of all – the customer himself. If the potential order isn't too large it may well give you enough information on which to base your credit-granting decision, but if the order is at all sizeable you would probably be wise to supplement the opinion of the salespeople with some of the other sources of credit information mentioned below.

What your salespeople can tell you

Your salespeople can identify the customer accurately: is it a limited company, partnership or sole trader? What is the firm's correct name and address? They can find out for you who authorizes payment of accounts and whether the customer has any special accounting requirements – ie order numbers to be quoted on invoices, extra copy invoices. All this helps you to invoice quickly and correctly and should reduce the number of queries and excuses for delayed payments.

Salespeople can make some assessment of the customer's ability to pay by ascertaining precisely the sort of business he is in and finding out how he gets paid by his customers. If, for example, he primarily supplies large companies, he may have no problems *getting* paid, but he may not be paid promptly. If he isn't, can he pay you on time?

How's business? is a common enough question for salespeople to ask conversationally of prospective customers, and it often gets them talking. Apart from revealing basic information on the firm's sales, turnover, number of employees, the customer may hint at business troubles and these could well set the alarm bells ringing.

Salespeople may be able to delve further too and discover whether the customer owns the business premises, and what assets he has in the form of vehicles, plant and machinery. And, from their visits, they should be in a position to judge from appearances how viable the business seems – are the premises well maintained or rundown? Is the location right? Do the staff appear happy and positive?

You will need to brief your salespeople thoroughly that they're collecting information for a dual purpose – sales and credit assessment. It will drum it in further if you ask salespeople to take a credit application form (see Figure 9) for the prospective customer to complete (leave space at the end for the salespeople to add their comments and recommendation).

Figure 9 Credit account application form

CREDIT ACCOUNT APPLICATION

Customer's full name:
Trading Address:
State whether *Limited Company, Partnership* or *Sole Trader:*
Number of employees:
Main activity:
Maximum credit required at any one time:
Present suppliers of competitive lines:

Name and address of two trade references (not associated companies):
    Reference 1

    Reference 2

Name and address of bankers:

TO BE COMPLETED BY LIMITED COMPANIES ONLY:
Registered Office Address:

When was the company formed?
Names of directors:
Issued paid-up capital:

TO BE COMPLETED BY ALL OTHER APPLICANTS:
Full name of proprietor/senior partner:
Home address:

How long has the business traded?
I/we apply for a credit account with (*your business name*) subject to the payment terms and other conditions set out overleaf

                Signed ....
                   (Authorised Signatory)

SALESPERSON'S COMMENTS AND RECOMMENDATION:

If orders are taken by telephone, instruct tele-sales staff to ascertain automatically the correct name of the company, its full address and whether it is a limited company, partnership or sole trader. This is probably all you can reasonably expect tele-sales staff to find out over the phone – although the more astute could be encouraged to engage in some of the gentle probing outlined above.

Making the most of trade references

Taking up a couple of trade references is now such a traditional method of checking out a new customer that it's really only of limited value as a base for an important financial decision. The customer expects you to do it and has the names and addresses of two suppliers ready and waiting. And, inevitably, he's only going to choose suppliers he knows will speak well of him. Also, trade references only actually tell you how the potential customer pays that particular supplier – which is not necessarily how he will pay you (many bad payers keep a few accounts up-to-date especially to use as references).

To get the most from trade references and at the same time to demonstrate that you have a businesslike attitude to credit-granting, vary the routine approach:

- **Ask for more than two references**. People invariably ask for two so the customer always keeps two up his sleeve – but there's no law that restricts the number of references you can request.
- **Ask different questions**. Standard questions like: How long have you known the customer? Are payments prompt, reasonable, poor? elicit standard answers. Try more searching questions, eg:
  - Is the trading style and address as shown correct?
  - Are you in any way associated with the company?
  - How long have you been trading with the company?
  - Are you currently trading with the company?
  - What is the maximum credit you extend to this firm in any one month?
  - What are your payment terms?
  - Compared with those terms are the customer's payments prompt, reasonable, slow or poor?

- Have you in the last six months had to take any final collection action against this company?

If there are any questions that are particularly relevant to your type of business, ask these too.

At the end of your request ask for any other relevant information that might assist your decision (and leave plenty of space for the answer!)

Do give some thought to the presentation of your request form. A tatty, photocopied document suggests that you consider this just a routine, fairly unimportant exercise – and the referee will see it in the same light. An attractively designed, well-presented form will make it appear a more serious request and will give your company a more professional image.

It's sometimes worth telephoning one of the firms given as a reference for an off-the-record chat. And don't be afraid to approach a competitor about a potential new customer. Often there is co-operation on credit because everyone has the same problems.

Bank status enquiries decoded

A reference from your potential customer's bank is likely to be more objective than a trade reference – which may well be given by a firm which *has* to be paid promptly because it supplies some essential component or suchlike. A bank reference is also likely to be more up-to-date than a credit status report (see next section). The reports produced by many credit reference agencies (especially the big firms) rely almost entirely on the last set of accounts filed, although more personalized reports will attempt to dig out the latest information available.

The problem with bank status enquiries, though, is that they contain very little information, and what they do is couched in gobbledegook. Unlike trade references they're not free either – they cost around £6 each.

The banks counter criticism with the fact that providing references places them in a somewhat invidious position: the bank has a responsibility to show its customer in the best possible light and also a responsibility to protect its own back where the customer's money is concerned.

Why then, given the confidential nature of the banker/customer contract, do banks give references at all? Because the law has determined that the bank's duty of secrecy can be breached under certain circumstances and one of the implied conditions of the banker/customer contract is that the bank will answer status enquiries directed to it, so long as the reply is being sent to another bank or a recognized credit institution.

Given the fine dividing line between an implied right (and duty) of disclosure, and the danger of a breach of confidentiality (and therefore a breach of contract for which the bank could be sued) the guarded lingo used in status reports is more understandable. Here's a translation.

Reports on companies

A status report on a company will usually begin: '*A respectably constituted private (or public) company*'. This doesn't mean the company is necessarily either respectable or creditworthy; it simply means the bank is satisfied that the company is properly registered in accordance with the Companies Acts.

The report will then go on to say something about the company's creditworthiness. This may be: '*Should prove good (occasionally undoubted) for normal business engagements/credit of £XXX a month*'. This is about the best you can get in the way of a reference. It implies a satisfactory company, not just from the point of view of the bank account, but also from the knowledge the bank has at the time the report was made.

'*Your figures are larger than we would normally expect to see*' probably indicates that transactions of the amount you were enquiring about would put a considerable strain on the customer's resources. It may just mean, however, that the company is new to the bank and not much information is available on it – although, if this is the case, the bank is likely to qualify the reference with '*new to this branch*' or something similar.

'*Would not enter into any commitment they could not see their way to fulfil*' is not so good and should be taken as a warning signal. It suggests that the bank knows that the company's financial situation is pretty tight, but that it has no reason to believe that the people controlling the business are anything but sound.

'*Resources fully committed*' means that you should be very wary. The customer is probably on or over its overdraft limit, and the bank is concerned that the firm would be unable to fulfil further commitments.

'*Unable to speak for your figures*' is about the worst possible reference you can have. It indicates that the bank has very little confidence in your customer.

Sometimes a reply will indicate that there are '*Charges registered*', usually in favour of the bank. This indicates that a debenture has been given, so that if the company fails, the debenture-holder has first call on the company's assets, which means that there may be nothing left for unsecured creditors.

Individuals, sole traders and partnerships

If satisfactory, references on individuals or unincorporated businesses will usually be prefaced: '*Respectable and trustworthy*' and continue in the same vein as the company reports. Sometimes you may find phrases like: '*Might require time to pay if called upon*' (perhaps where an individual is guaranteeing a lease or third-party borrowing), or, '*Known to us as the director of a company customer.*'

If you receive different replies to the above on either companies or individuals, ask your own bank manager to interpret them for you, or speak to the bank sending the report if he can't.

There is no point, incidentally, making an enquiry for an amount out of proportion to the value of expected orders. A company which '*should prove good*' for credit of £10,000 a month may not be a satisfactory risk for total credit of £100,000. And there is little point asking for references at all if you propose to allow unlimited credit.

Credit status reports

Commissioning a credit status report on a company from a specialized credit reference agency should give you a much more detailed picture of your prospective customers and their creditworthiness than you will get from the other sources mentioned above.

Although the many credit reference agencies which supply them vary considerably in what they charge, credit status reports needn't be expensive – between around £20 and £40 to buy from a smaller credit reference agency – and it can be money well spent if a large amount of credit is at stake. Status reports needn't just be *credit* status reports, though. You may like to check out your suppliers, particularly if a long-term contract is involved – or your competitors to help determine your marketing policy. Credit reference agencies say that companies often check out themselves too.

This is the information a status report should tell you: the company's name and registered office address; when it was formed; what it does; capital structure and shareholders; directors and company secretary. It should give you a potted history of the business in a few lines and should then briefly analyse the financial position, relating it to previous years and to the current climate in the particular industry and/or the country (if an export account is involved). It should pay particular regard to the liquidity and external borrowing, trade creditors against trade debtors and whether the directors have loans. It should also comment on any unusual charges on file such as charges registered in the names of directors, shareholders or members of the same group. Next, the credit reference agency should comment on the credit risk involved. This should be related to the amount of credit you are seeking to extend – for instance if the potential customer has sales of £250,000, a credit facility of £750 should be no problem, but £7,500 might need a lot more justification.

When it comes to telling you what you really want to know, ie can the company generate sufficient cash to pay its debts? some agencies tell you straight out, but with others you may need to read between the lines. For instance, if the report shows that the company has a turnover of £100,000 but that £70,000 of this is tied up in stock and a further £70,000 is already owed to creditors then you can see the company has problems: unless it can shift the bulk of its stock, it is likely to pay only its most important creditors promptly.

Some reports include an analysis of payments to suppliers – useful since they show the exact amounts involved – while others detail the customer's average payment time – an aid to your forward cash planning.

Figure 10 Credit status report

13th December, 1988

REGENCY REPORT

SUBJECT   SPRINGS SMOKED SALMON

STATEMENT OF ACCOUNT
REFERENCE NO.   STAT 3323

We searched our index but could find no listing for a limited liability entity Springs Smoked Salmon Limited.

Our long range enquiries established that this is in fact a non-limited concern the proprietor being a G.D. Harris. It is a well established firm and is engaged in the curing of salmon and the selling of same to hotels and restaurants around the Sussex area.

We have confirmed that the subject operates out of premises at The Springs, Edburton, telephone number Poynings 338 and believe that this may also be the private residence of the proprietor G.D. Harris but we have not been able to confirm whether this is correct or not.

As part of our enquiries we searched the records of a leading Commercial Data Base in the name of subject but found nothing registered.

We also made a search of a national Consumer Credit Bureau's records in the name of G.D. Harris but once again found nothing registered.

Our own in-house records show nothing detrimental regarding the payment of accounts and we have not been asked to collect from the subject of enquiry.

We contacted a selection of hotels and restaurants in the Sussex area and can say that 99% of those contacted referred us to "Springs" for the best smoked salmon in the area as well as the quality of service etc.

As the subject is not a limited company it is not therefore required to file accounts and we are therefore reliant on any information that can be gleaned from discreet enquiries but we would gauge from the information to hand that the subject of enquiry would appear to be a well thought of concern with no adverse information registered against it and should be considered therefore a good trading risk.

The foregoing information is given in strict confidence at your request without responsibility or liability on our part in respect of its contents or any matters or actions arising therefrom and is not to be disclosed or divulged to any person, firm or company outside your immediate organisation. This report should not be used in isolation but in conjunction with information from other sources available to you.

Yours faithfully,

for REGENCY CONSULTANTS

(Reproducted by kind permission of Regency Consultants, Chester)

A certain mystique surrounds the workings of credit reference agencies – shades of dirty undercover work? – but the way they collect their information is actually surprisingly straightforward. Information from the files at the Companies Registration Office (see address in Appendix A) forms the basis of the status report. This, of course, is something you can get yourself (for details see Chapter 7).

But agencies go further: checks are made at the Registry of County Court Judgements, on winding-up orders and recorded HP payments. Directors' addresses are usually checked against the Electoral Register. Some agencies ask existing suppliers to the company for an opinion too.

Where a large credit risk is involved, or where the situation warrants it for other reasons, discreet enquiries are made locally: the police are sometimes prepared to say if a company is known to them for any reason; the local employment office can be a source of information, and the fire officer who inspected the premises sometimes has a story to tell. Now and again it's necessary to involve an enquiry agent (they are usually retired police people).

Searches at local level can often throw light on a rumoured situation which is not reflected in the accounts. For example, one company probing the affairs of a prospective customer, rumoured to be in trouble because it hadn't paid its rates bill, was reassured when the credit agency's checks revealed that the customer was perfectly viable, but was withholding its rates in protest against the local authority's refusal to grant planning permission for a new headquarters building because the authority was trying to force the firm to move to a new trading estate nearby.

There are many hundreds of firms supplying credit status reports. They range from the big boys like Dun & Bradstreet and CCN to much smaller firms. They are listed in *Yellow Pages* under 'Credit Investigation Services', but it might be safer to ask one of the following organizations to give you the names of their member-firms in your particular area: The Credit Services Association, The Institute of Credit Management (addresses in Appendix A).

Some agencies, usually the larger ones, maintain ongoing files on companies, so can turn out a status report from the file very quickly. But what you gain in speed you may sacrifice in results. Apart from there being no guarantee that it's bang up to date, a standard report on file might not be flexible enough to highlight the facts that particularly interest *you*, whereas a report specially commissioned from scratch should do so – provided you liaise closely with the agency and tell them frankly about your business and what you want to know.

The large agencies too tend to sell credit status reports on a subscription basis which makes them very expensive to buy as one-offs (if they are even prepared to provide them on this basis) but less per report if you need a good many. A good smaller agency is a better bet if you only want an occasional credit reference report and a personalized service.

On-line and related credit reference services

If speed and ease of access are your main criteria when deciding whether to grant credit facilities you can subscribe to one of the growing number of services (Dun & Bradstreet, Jordans, for example) which provide credit status reports on-line.

If you have Prestel or Telecom Gold, instant credit reports on over a million companies are available on screen from the computer database of a firm called Infocheck. The information you'll receive includes the firm's most up-to-date filed accounts, up to four years' worth of accounts to review; up to 75 ratios (many of which you won't require) plus an opinion on the firm's creditworthiness.

You can either key in the first ten digits of the name of the company you require, or its registration number – use the latter wherever possible, because there can be all sorts of problems if the company has a long name (you can't abbreviate) or starts with a common word like INTERNATIONAL.

If you *don't* have a computer, but would like an on-line facility, Dun & Bradstreet offer the use of their massive computer database via the telephone. Any multi-frequency telephone will do (the kind that sounds a tone when you press the buttons).

You first have to sign a contract with D & B. The charging system is based on the number of units you're likely to use.

Once signed up, you telephone DunsVoice. Then, by tapping the relevant numbers on your handset, enter your subscription number and the first seven digits of the registration number of the firm you wish to investigate. The computer's female voice takes you through a 'yes' and 'no' technique (you press 9 for yes, 6 for no) until you get the data you require.

These services will certainly make your credit control operation quicker and easier, but bear in mind again that database reports will be based mainly on the latest filed accounts which inevitably don't paint the most up-to-date picture (volatile firms could now be doing very much better – or very much worse), and computer reports need to rely on standard guidelines to arrive at creditworthiness conclusions. This is where specially commissioned one-off status reports can score. They use human analysts who are able to look beyond the figures to come up with a realistic assessment. A company making losses, for instance, is not *necessarily* a credit risk, whereas a company making big profits could be a *payments* risk due to lack of liquidity.

Case Story 6

Credit reports give you an edge in negotiations too

A small northern firm was being courted by a much larger company based in the south of England to work in partnership on one particular deal. The northern directors took the precaution of commissioning a credit status report on this possible partner. The report revealed the not uninteresting information that two of the firm's directors had resigned at the same time six months previously.

At the subsequent meeting between the two companies, the northerners asked why the two directors had suddenly pulled out. The southerners were completely taken aback. They were totally amazed that the northern company should know their dark and intimate secrets and quite at a loss as to how to answer the question. This was very much to the northern firm's advantage as from that moment on the whole tenor of the discussion changed with the larger company abandoning its previously rather high-handed and decidedly patronizing stance to its smaller compatriot, and negotiations were conducted on a much more equal footing.

How does your firm rate credit-wise?

Credit reference agencies might be running checks on you at this very moment. If you've been tardy about filing your latest accounts or if you are withholding or delaying payments for any reason – because you think a supplier has done you down, or just as normal business practice to help your cash flow – it's worth bearing in mind that this could actually have a disproportionately serious effect on your ability to do business in the future.

The potential supplier of a manufacturing company was advised by its credit reporting agency that the manufacturing company was insolvent. In fact the company was trading very successfully and had been doing so for three and a half years, although from an accounting point of view it made a minimal loss of £30 in the first year. However, for some reason the executive director had 'forgotten' to file any but the first year's accounts and the credit agency had based its opinion on these accounts alone. It is an offence, of course, for directors to neglect to file accounts with the Companies Registration Office – 1,558 directors were convicted of it in 1989.

Why you must get the name right

Common business courtesy, let alone common sense, should make you ensure that you get the names of your customers and suppliers totally correct at the outset. Yet many firms are very sloppy about this. Common errors are to add 'Limited' where it doesn't belong, or drop it from a title where it does; to abbreviate words which should be spelt out, or reverse the order of words – particularly when the title of the company contains names and initials. It's worth remembering that all limited company information is held in strictly alphabetical order which means J. Smith Ltd falls among the Js and many thousands of entries away from Smith, J Ltd or John Smith Ltd.

Everybody, of course, *thinks* they know who they are supplying to, or buying from, and a lack of knowledge of the real identity goes unnoticed in the majority of transactions which, fortunately, are concluded to the satisfaction of both parties. It's only when things go wrong that the question of identity becomes one of paramount importance. You can't sue a company unless you know its correct name, and if you ask a collection agency to chase up a debt for you, they're unlikely to waive their charges if they go to work on the wrong company.

Case Story 7 illustrates just how badly you can come unstuck by not taking that little bit of extra care.

Case Story 7

What's in a name?

Careless Company Ltd obtained a massive order from 30th Century Whatsits Ltd. After Careless Company Ltd had applied for, and received, a glowing credit report it processed the order. Some 90 days from invoicing, though, no payment had been received. After a few weeks of promised payments, nothing materialized and Careless Company's credit manager

---

called his debt collection agency, dictating the customer details over the phone.

The agent obtained the registered office address of Thirtieth Century Whatsits Ltd from its microfilmed company index and issued a writ.

Thirtieth Century Whatsits Ltd went berserk. In all their years of trading they had never been sued, and Thirtieth Century's purchasing department had no record of an order from Careless Company Ltd. Lawyers were called in and acted promptly to prevent judgment being obtained.

Eventually the reason for the confusion emerged: Careless Company Ltd had made a contract with 30th Century Whatsits Ltd, but all the way along the line had recorded the name as 'Thirtieth'. Nobody had realized that there were two limited liability companies with the same phonetic name, one using words, the other figures. The fact that the registered office address was different from the trading address rang no alarm bells as this is common practice.

This little slip-up cost Careless Company Ltd a great deal of money (this is a true story but the names have been changed). They had granted credit based on information relating to a different company. 30th Century Whatsits Ltd were in liquidation so Careless Company Ltd had lost all the costs of the sale and the profit. They also had to pay Thirtieth Century Whatsits' legal costs on top of their own. They were probably lucky not to end up facing a claim for damages as well!

5

Getting debts paid promptly

An unpaid debt is a loan being financed by your company. Have you worked out how much such 'loans' are costing you each year? According to one estimate, small firms in Britain are owed more than £100 billion due to late payment of debts. A staggering figure. And it means that many companies are prevented from achieving their full potential because, instead of using borrowed money to develop and grow their businesses, they are having to borrow money just to fund their sales ledger.

Figure 11   What debts cost

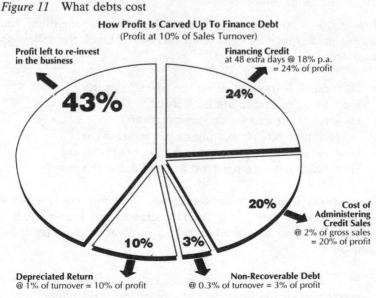

How Profit Is Carved Up To Finance Debt
(Profit at 10% of Sales Turnover)

Profit left to re-invest in the business

43%

Financing Credit
at 48 extra days @ 18% p.a.
= 24% of profit

24%

20%

Cost of Administering Credit Sales
@ 2% of gross sales
= 20% of profit

10%   **3%**

Depreciated Return
@ 1% of turnover = 10% of profit

Non-Recoverable Debt
@ 0.3% of turnover = 3% of profit

Source: Intrum Justita

British firms wait on average 78 days for their bills to be paid, despite the fact that stated payment terms are usually 30 days. And the cost of financing that extra 48 days credit is expensive. Credit management group, Intrum Justita, estimates that it's equivalent to 5.7 per cent of turnover – more than 50 per cent of net profit – when you take into account the combined costs of financing the credit with borrowed money, the extra administration involved, the cost of depreciation over the 48 days, and allowing for debts that can't be recovered.

It is claimed too that British companies with competitors in Europe will be put at a disadvantage by our poor payments discipline (for details of how other countries compare see Appendix B).

Many people think that something positive should be done to pressurize poor payers to cough up more promptly – the bigger the company the longer it appears to take to pay its bill. The initiatives that have been taken are detailed in the next chapter.

Given the national situation, every business needs to place great emphasis on its debt collection procedures on the principle that those who shout loudest get the best results.

Check out your credit control

How good is *your* control of credit? If this is something you haven't given much thought to so far, ask yourself the following questions:

- How much is owed to us on the Sales Ledger?
- How much of that figure is overdue?
- How much do we owe on our overdraft?
- What is that actually costing us per month/year?
- How much did we write off in bad debts last year?
- How much have we reserved for bad debts this year?

The answers may point up weaknesses in your credit control function and will give you some indication of just how much it is really costing you to extend credit to customers. Now try these questions:

- How does a customer get credit from us? Does he fill in a credit application form, send in an order or telephone?

- Is there a level at which we don't extend credit?
- Do we ask for cash with order for small amounts?
- What steps, if any, do we take to determine a customer's ability to pay *before* extending credit?
- What do we do to collect the money due to us?
- What are our final sanctions against a customer who owes us money?
- How effective are these procedures in practice?

Why you need a credit control policy

Operating a poor credit control policy is a costly business. It means you pay higher interest than you need on your overdraft or fail to earn interest on a deposit account. Also, the more chase-up letters and telephone calls made, the higher the costs and the greater the amount of time spent by staff who could be employed on more productive tasks.

Your credit control policy should lay down which companies are allowed credit and how much; should state when invoices, statements and follow-up letters are sent out, and should lay down the plan of action to be adopted if these procedures don't produce the cash.

Customers and credit

Credit is normally extended to customers for one reason only, that of attracting higher and more profitable sales. Every customer's credit should be reviewed regularly with this in mind.

If you make a lot of credit transactions you probably have a sales day book in which sales details are entered in sequence by transaction and a debtors ledger in which each customer who is allowed credit has an individual account (or you keep the equivalent information on computer). But do you have enough information on each customer?

For the efficient collection of debts you need to know as much as possible about the customer's payment pattern and procedures, and to keep a note of all your dealings with him. This record is perhaps best kept on a separate card index (if you operate a manual, rather than a computer system) to avoid cluttering up the debtors ledger. It should show the customer's name, address, account number, credit limit with the date on which it was agreed or changed, who in the customer's company looks after your invoices, the customer company's cut-off date for processing invoices and any other relevant points. Then there should be ample space for recording brief details of all telephone and written contact relating to the account. Over a period, a clear picture builds up of how your debtor operates and this helps determine the best approaches to adopt. It is also invaluable should credit staff change or fall ill.

Analysing your debtors

Once you know precisely how much money is owing, for how long, from which customers, you need to prepare an 'aged debtor analysis' viz:

Figure 12 Aged debtors analysis

MONTHS OVERDUE

ACCOUNT	3+	2	1	Actual overdue	Not yet due	Total
	£	£	£	£	£	£
A						
B						
C						
D						
etc						
TOTALS						

This is one of the fundamental monitoring tools Chapter 1 advised you to keep on a monthly basis. It not only helps you allocate priorities to your debt collection activity but informs you of the total amount of money tied up in debtors.

The pattern can be compared with the same period the previous year to see if things are getting better or worse. The trend from month to month is a useful indicator of either changing performance of credit control or the changing pattern of customer behaviour. When a particular customer moves out of line, this indicates possible trouble and should be investigated quickly. Sales people should be alerted too in case it is necessary to stop supplies.

Implementing a collection programme

You need to lay down a programme for collecting debts and to work it consistently. That way it becomes an integral part of the firm's activities and it shows your customers you mean business.

For a company operating on 30-day terms of payment, a typical programme might go like this:

Day 1: send invoice
Day 31: send statement
Day 41: send first reminder letter
Day 51: send second reminder letter
Day 58: start telephone chasing
Day 65: final action (stop supplies, debt referred to debt collection agency/solicitor, county court action initiated, statutory demand for payment sent)

Before examining each of these stages in more detail it should be said that the programme outlined above is a very conventional one – corners can be cut to speed things up.

First, why 30 days? Payment within 30 days from the date of invoice seems to have become some sort of sacred cow. There's no reason why it shouldn't be 20 days, 14 days or whatever you choose. Some firms are now introducing terms like 'payment on invoice'. They don't expect the customer to deal with the invoice the day it's received but it allows the firm to start the collection programme that much quicker.

There is no law either which says you must send your debtors statements or written reminders. Some companies don't bother with them at all – once the payment period is up they switch straight to telephone chasing.

Let's now examine the stages of the collection programme in more detail:

- **Invoices**. Send them out as soon as possible. Don't wait until the end of the month, or even later as many firms do. Ideally send your invoices when you despatch the goods or perform the service (but consider the VAT – see page 65). Always get proof of delivery and, if possible, proof of posting when sending goods by post – it's the oldest trick in the book for those trying to wriggle out of paying to say the goods have never arrived. In the none-too-distant future, paper invoices are likely to be a thing of the past as 'paperless' invoices which are transmitted direct from your computer screen to your customer's screen take over. Electronic Data Interchange (EDI for short) is already being used in day-to-day business dealings by many large organizations, and some of them are beginning to say they will do business only with suppliers prepared to adopt EDI. For information on EDI contact SITPRO (see Appendix A).

- **Statements**. Again, send them out promptly – as soon as possible after the expiry of the stated payment period. Faxing, rather than posting, can make them seem more urgent and the rubber stamping or attaching of a self-adhesive 'overdue' or 'have you forgotten?' sticker may also speed things along.
- **Written reminders**. Devise two standard letters to be sent out at defined intervals (see page 95), the first perhaps a week or so after the statement. Set a deadline for payment – say, seven to ten days after the first reminder which, if ignored, triggers the second letter. Sending the second letter by recorded delivery can make more impact.
- **Telephone contact**. Don't waste any more time with written reminders if you've heard nothing a week to ten days after the second letter went out. Start the telephone chase (see page 96). First, it is necessary to establish that there's no dispute – that the customer has received the order and is not dissatisfied with what is provided. Then it's a matter of getting him to commit himself to making a payment, and going back to him immediately, if the payment doesn't arrive when anticipated, for another commitment.

  At this stage you, the boss, might get results by telephoning your opposite number in the customer company and gently asking 'is there a problem, I'm told you haven't paid our bill'.
- **Final action**. Your first option is to *stop supplies* if the customer still doesn't pay and his contract is for regular and ongoing deliveries. Withholding supplies, however, is a potentially risky thing to do if there are any number of people in your line of business, as the customer may take his custom elsewhere and be lost to you for ever. Maybe it's possible just to withhold credit facilities but continue to supply cash on

delivery until the outstanding debt is settled. If withholding supplies/credit doesn't produce the cash you can either:

- *Take the debtor to court*: many firms are reluctant to do this either out of fear of offending customers (but who wants them if they don't pay?) or because of the legal fees involved. But you don't necessarily need a solicitor if the case is straightforward and the amount is under £1,000 – you can sue it yourself through the arbitration procedure in the county court
- *Send a Statutory Demand for Payment* (see Chapter 6)
- *Call in a debt collection agency* (see Chapter 6)
- *Pass the debt to a solicitor for legal action.*

Once you've formulated your policy, stick to it rigidly. Customers get to know who means business when it comes to prompt payment. This is especially true in large organizations where invoices are processed by clerks. These staff quickly learn which companies press them for payment, and which companies don't bother – and they tend to set their priorities accordingly.

Your own staff, of course, must be totally *au fait* with your policy and procedures. It's vital, too, that customers know and understand your payment terms. They should be part of your Terms and Conditions of Sale. An explanation of the different terminology used for payment terms is given in Chapter 3.

Terms and Conditions of Sale

Your Terms and Conditions cover much more than your payment terms. They form the basis of your contract with customers so it's important to get them right. How are yours? Do they state *clearly* the grounds on which you are prepared to do business, and will they stand up *legally* should a dispute arise?

Combining these twin objectives isn't that easy. If you ask a lawyer to draw up a set of Terms and Conditions which cover every legal point and every situation which could conceivably arise, you're likely to end up with an interminably long and complex document, intelligible only to another lawyer. And if *you* don't understand your terms and conditions how on earth are you going to explain them to a customer?

Examine your own Terms and Conditions – do they need simplifying? The clause on payment, for instance, just needs to say something like: 'Payment is strictly net and is due 30 days after the date of invoice'. It could well go on: 'The company reserves the right to charge interest on overdue accounts at three per cent over the minimum lending rate.' (The pros and cons of charging interest on overdue accounts are examined on page 101).

No matter how legally binding your Terms and Conditions are, or how cleverly drawn up, they won't be any use unless your customers know about them and accept them before entering into the deal. It's no good for instance, just printing them on the back of your invoices – you might not be able to enforce them in the event of a dispute since your customer could legitimately claim he didn't know of their existence when he contracted to do business with you.

Print your Terms and Conditions on the back of your order form, with a clause on the front saying 'We have read your terms and conditions and agree to abide by them,' and get the customer to sign this. Those who work by quotation might find it safer to print their Terms and Conditions on the back of their standard quotation form and draw attention to them on the front: 'This quotation is submitted subject to the standard terms and conditions overleaf.'

Your potential customer may have conditions of *purchase* and this gives him the opportunity to discover whether the two sets of conditions match up. *You* should make sure, too, that you check your customer's conditions of purchase when you receive the order. Only if there is no conflict in the respective conditions should you acknowledge the order and your confirmation of it is the final act in making the contract between you a legally enforceable deal.

How to write collection letters

A survey conducted a few years ago showed that 94 per cent of businesses use letters to collect overdue accounts but only 18 per cent considered them effective.

Why? Mainly because reminder letters are too 'nice'. They don't encourage firms to take the demand seriously. You've seen (or might even be using yourself) letters with the Uriah Heep touch: 'I do indeed appreciate that the present financial climate is difficult but would welcome your attention to our account . . .', 'Whilst regretting the need to do so, draw your attention to a matter which we are sure will be of mutual concern . . .' (this one is sometimes so oblique that it shies away from even mentioning the amount!) And they end: 'Assuring you of our best attention at all times.'

Of course it's natural to wish to retain the customer's goodwill, but these letters are not businesslike and don't project the image of an efficient firm. The fact is that if your customer has seen your Terms and Conditions, he is in breach of the contract between you if he fails to pay within the allotted time.

Every letter costs money, so get your message across in a way that's calculated to get a response. Forget the archaic phrases, forget the traditional jargon like: 'If you have paid within the last ten days please ignore this letter and accept our apologies for troubling you.' Although the postal service is none too hot, this statement suggests that your firm's cash collection is so bad that it takes ten days to realize the customer has paid – and invites him to take even longer.

Keep the letters short and to the point. Say what you mean and mean what you say. If you intend to stop supplies, stop them; if you say you'll sue, sue. Threats which aren't carried out destroy your credibility.

As we said earlier, two letters are enough before switching to telephone collection. (One company used five – what's more each contained a reference: 'No 1 of 5', 'No 2 of 5' etc so debtors merely waited to see what 'No 5 of 5' had to say!)

Figure 13   Examples of collection letters that work

First reminder

Dear Sirs,

OVERDUE ACCOUNT £_____

The above account is overdue for payment. Please pay this sum immediately, or advise us of any reason for non-payment.

Unless we hear from you within ten days of today's date, we shall suspend further deliveries.

Yours faithfully,

Final letter

BREACH OF TERMS OF SALE
FINAL NOTICE

Dear Sirs,

OVERDUE ACCOUNT £_____

The above sum remains outstanding and requests for payment have been ignored.

Supplies are now suspended and unless payment is made within the next seven days we shall pass the matter to our debt collection agency/ issue proceedings against you without further notice.

Yours faithfully,

Give some thought to the design and appearance of your collection letters – they are part of your business image after all. How will they look to the recipient? Would they make *you* pay? Borders in different colours and boxes saying: BREACH OF TERMS OF SALE or OVERDUE ACCOUNT add a sense of urgency.

Debt collection by telephone

Chasing up debts by telephone is a selling job. Yes, selling – it's all about persuading your customers that they should pay *you* rather than someone else.

Few businesses would expect untrained staff to sell by telephone, yet many regard telephone collection as a 'spare-time' activity for junior staff. Isn't your cash flow too important to be put into unskilled hands?

Telephone chasers are expected to collect from both customers who can pay now but would rather pay later, and customers with genuine cash flow problems.

The first category, on being telephoned, is likely to make vague promises: 'A cheque as soon as possible', 'You're on the next computer run'. They will not change their payment pattern and will regard the call as no more important than the many similar calls they receive every day – unless the telephone chaser knows how to be very persuasive.

Customers in the second category are a different problem. Here, the chaser needs to establish that the cash flow problem is genuine, how serious it is, what the customer is doing about it and what other creditors are doing about it. The telephone chaser has to know how to ask the right questions in the right way so that decisions can be taken, and maybe how to enter into negotiations.

The person you ask to do your debt-chasing over the telephone thus needs to be someone with knowledge of your business, someone who can be both polite and assertive when necessary with good telephone technique. And someone to whom you are prepared to give considerable responsibility.

It's not what you say, it's the way that you say it

Assuming that you have a debt chaser with the requisite knowledge of your business, consider his or her telephone manner. You don't want to upset customers but you want your call to be taken seriously and not just seen as a polite reminder service. Is your debt-chaser someone with a smile-in-the-voice which can become the hint of a growl?

People should speak neither too fast nor too slow – too rapidly and the other party might only notice the rate at which they speak; too slow and the listener will be irritated into anticipating what is coming next. Enunciation is more important when talking on the telephone since the other party can't watch the lips, and experts claim that a low-pitched, rather than a high-pitched, voice projects and carries better – it's also more pleasant to listen to. A voice with a rising inflection towards the end of a sentence is more exciting than a flat monotone.

Telephone debt chasers need to prepare carefully before they call. They must have all the facts and figures at their fingertips, and be sure they are correct – challenging the accuracy of the information is a common ploy of would-be debt evaders. Chasers need to keep control of the conversation and anticipate likely diversionary tactics and excuses by those able but unwilling to settle debts promptly.

A good technique to get a commitment from a debtor is to ask a logical series of questions all of which can only be answered by a 'yes' or a 'no' to lead the debtor to the point where he will find it difficult to refuse to settle the account. For example: 'Can I confirm that you received the goods in August?', 'I believe you also received our invoice?', 'Do you agree that there is an outstanding balance of £x now due for payment?', 'We can expect your cheque then?', 'What date will that be?'. The conversation *must* end with agreement to some positive action.

Responsibility with authority

When asking a member of staff to collect money by telephone you are giving them considerable responsibility, but do you give them the appropriate *authority*? Do they have the authority to place a customer 'on stop'? The authority to negotiate? The authority to say 'We will sue'?

If the answer is no, they have responsibility without authority which means they cannot be as effective as they could be. Knowledge and skill can be learnt, but authority has to be delegated. If the person responsible for telephone collection is too junior to be given authority then he or she is too junior for the responsibility.

Define your objectives

Your objective in chasing debts by telephone should be to collect the money due, promptly and at economic cost. Too often this objective is not clearly defined and therefore seldom achieved. The same calls are made regularly to the same customers month after month. The customer knows the call is coming and knows that by making a further 'on-account' payment he can keep you off his back for a further month. In this situation the collector's approach is often reduced to asking 'How much are you going to pay this time?'.

Although this approach does produce money, it's what the customer decides to pay, not what is due. Result: your cash flow isn't as good as it should and could be.

If the customer is having genuine problems, though, it's sensible to be a bit more flexible. Here *some* money really is better than none and you build up strong customer loyalty if you help another firm over a temporary bad patch.

Discounts for early settlement

One way to induce customers to pay more promptly is to offer them a discount if they settle their bills early. This is supposed to be both a reward to the customer for honouring the debt quickly and compensation for the additional interest they will have to pay on their overdraft because of early settlement.

At first sight this may seem a good solution to payment problems, but it's not really such a sensible idea. Customers are sometimes known to take the discount but still delay payment, and the interest charges on a discount can be very expensive as far as your business is concerned since discounts need to be fairly sizeable if they are to act as real inducements.

This is the equation you use to work out the interest on a discount:

$$I = R \times \frac{365}{d} \quad \text{where}: \quad \begin{aligned} I &= \text{Annual interest rate} \\ R &= \text{Discount rate} \\ d &= \text{Number of days paid} \\ &\quad \text{earlier due to discount} \end{aligned}$$

If, for instance, you were offering a discount of 3¾ per cent to customers settling in seven days, rather than the 60 days normally taken, the figures would look like this:

$$3.75 \times \frac{365}{53} = 25.8\%$$

(ie 60 days normal terms – seven days allowed for discount)

As you are unlikely to be paying 25.8 per cent on the money you are borrowing from the bank, this puts you out of pocket. Even if you have no borrowings, and the money is your own, you would have to be making 25.8 per cent return on capital employed before this discount is worth giving. As the UK average return on capital employed is below 18 per cent you would need to be pretty efficient!

The moral is: don't give discounts of this size for early settelement – but always take them!

The size of discount you would need to offer to accelerate payment by 50 days and to equate with current overdraft interest rates would be about two per cent. This is unlikely to be enough to tempt your customers. All in all, waiting for payment is cheaper than offering a cash discount.

Case Story 8

Sexist trick

Here's a little trick you might like to try if you sell to the general public and customers are not responding to your requests for payment. If the debtor is male, send a statement for twice the right amount. He's likely to respond instantly to correct the figure! If your debtor is female, send a statement for the amount less, say, five per cent. She's likely to pay at once, hoping you won't discover the mistake!

Credit control courses

If you think your company's handling of credit control and debt collection could do with a brush-up, consider going on a short training course. Several organizations run them and many courses take place in venues other than London. Here are five organizations (addresses in Appendix A) which run either half or one-day courses which have been recommended by the National Training Index. Course organizers: Shaws Linton; Dun & Bradstreet; Institute of Credit Management; Chartered Institute of Management Accountants; Mobile Training and Exhibitions Ltd.

6

Hitting the slow payers

The owner of a paper recycling business, asked how he coped with slow payers replied without hesitation: 'I send one of my 40ft articulated lorries round to the customer's premises and park it across the main gate so that no one can get in or out. And there it stays until I've got my money – it's never failed yet'

This chapter is not advocating such drastic measures. Apart from the fact that the Administration of Justice Act makes it an offence to harass people for payment (and this might well be construed as harassment), we don't all possess articulated vehicles.

But this chap has the right idea. Late payment is too easily taken for granted. Show that you mean business when customers are holding onto your money for unnecessarily long periods, not by being pushy but by using one of the several legitimate methods available to extract cash outlined below.

Charging interest

One stick to wave at your late payers is the threat of levying an interest charge on the amount owing from the date the account becomes overdue. This also enables you to recoup some of the extra costs incurred by long-standing debts.

However, you can only charge your customers interest if you have incorporated a clause in your Terms and Conditions of Sale (see previous chapter) which states that you claim the right to levy interest at x per cent over the bank lending rate on accounts not paid within a stated period. The usual rate of interest charged is around three per cent above bank base rate.

Where you can claim interest automatically, without the need of any clause, is if you have to sue for a debt. Here, you have a statutory right to claim interest at 15 per cent per annum from the date on which payment became due. If, for example, you sue for £1,500 at 90 days overdue, you can claim an additional £55.47 in interest.

Many smaller firms, though, are shy of enforcing clauses which entitle them to charge interest, thinking this will cause too much ill-feeling. Also, it's not uncommon for late paying customers to settle the debt, but minus the interest, and firms don't usually consider it's worth the trouble of pursuing customers through the courts just for a bit of interest which might only total a few pounds.

Given the UK's poor payment record (see Chapter 5), interest on overdue accounts has been the subject of much discussion over the last few years, culminating in a campaign to introduce legislation which would entitle businesses to have an automatic right to claim interest on all overdue accounts.

This is favoured by a large number of smaller businesses since they see it as giving them the clout they need to demand – and receive – interest payments on overdue accounts. It would also quantify the amount of interest that could be charged.

Opponents of a new law claim that it will be enforced by the large companies against the small, and the small against the very small but that few small companies would have the courage to enforce it against the very big.

And, argue the opponents, why introduce legislation when the right to charge interest already exists. It's not a new law that's needed, but a new attitude – ie businesses need to establish clearly their terms of payment, set up proper account collection systems and stick to them without fear or favour.

Mrs Thatcher's Conservative government, while acknowledging the strains on cash flow felt by smaller firms as a result of late payment, stopped short of legislation, confining itself instead to advocating a code of fair payment practice which is contained in the practical guide to suppliers and purchasers, *Prompt Payment Please*.

Most of our European trading partners, do, however, have legislation which allows interest to be claimed (although it is not always enforced), and the debate in Britain might well be resolved if the draft proposals of an EC directive become accepted. This incorporates an obligation to pay for goods and services within 45 days and an automatic obligation to pay interest from the first day after the payment deadline.

Debt collection agencies

Once your own internal debt collection efforts are exhausted it's worth considering placing unpaid debts in the hands of a professional debt collection agency as an intermediate stage before resorting to the legal process.

Collecting money through the courts can be time-consuming and costly so the fewer debts you have to recover this way, the better. And agencies can often be more successful than solicitors as this story illustrates: a magazine publisher trying to collect £2,000 from a slippery advertiser put the matter into the hands of his solicitor after going through all the usual procedures. Nothing happened for six months so the publisher called in a collection agency as a last resort. A few weeks later the debt was paid. Just to rub salt into the wound, the agency's fee was far lower than the solicitor's bill.

You might feel reluctant to involve a professional debt collector for fear of damaging relationships with customers, and because of the slightly grubby image that attaches itself to those whose business it is to extract money from people who don't want to pay. But these shouldn't be real problems if the agency you choose is reputable. Established agencies don't operate by sending in the heavies to make the debtor 'an offer he can't refuse'. The techniques they have evolved for collecting debts are quite simple and straightforward but tried and tested over the years. True, your customers might resent the fact that you've called in an agency to do your dirty work, but don't you resent the fact that the customer is hanging onto *your* money? The agency's intervention is thus likely to encourage these ordinary debtors to pay up – it also warns the professional debtor that you mean business.

Whether an agency can help or not, though, does depend on the 'quality' of the debts you ask it to collect. Good quality, in the words of one agency director means 'current, clean and collectable'. The older the debt the harder it is to collect, and the agency is unlikely to be successful if you and the customer are in dispute. Ideally, passing debts through to an agency should be built into your collection programme (see Chapter 5) with unpaid debts handed over as soon as your own chasing procedures are exhausted.

A debt collection agency, though, needn't be just a dumping ground for old debts. If your trading goes in peaks and troughs, using an agency's resources to provide extra collection effort if your own collection staff are overloaded could be money well spent in terms of the extra amount of working capital it will release.

Agencies collect debts by letter, telephone, and, if the debt is sizeable, agency staff may make personal visits to the debtor's premises. A good agency will try to collect without resorting to law. Inevitably, this isn't always possible but the agency should always review the situation with you, the client, before initiating legal action. If the debt is under £1,000 you may well prefer to pursue it yourself through the county court small claims procedure (see next chapter). If the debt is larger, or needs a solicitor because it is complicated, it is often sensible to let the agency handle it since agencies usually work closely with solicitors who specialize in debt collection cases. Apart from saving your time, this could well increase your chances of success in a court action. Some uncollectable debts are just not worth pursuing and should be written off; the agency's experience can guide you as to which these are and thus prevent you suing blindly.

How agencies charge

Some of the larger agencies work on a *voucher* system. Clients buy books of vouchers and when they want to use the debt collection service, just send in a voucher together with details of the debt. It's a neat idea but it does mean you are tying up your money by paying in advance for a service you might only use over quite a long period.

Most agencies charge by *commission*, ie they take a percentage of the amount of money they actually collect. Commission charges vary between agency and agency, and according to the age, value and number of debts you pass to them, so charges are always the subject of negotiation with the client. They range from somewhere around one per cent of the amount collected on debts for large amounts of money, to anywhere up and above ten per cent of the amount collected where the debt is small.

Don't be tempted to opt for an agency just because it charges the lowest commission. Performance is more important than the commission rate. If, for instance, agency A is charging you three per cent and agency B only one per cent but agency A collects 85 per cent of what's due and agency B only 60 per cent then agency A is the better deal. For example:

Debts of £20,000

Agency A		Agency B	
Collects	£17,000	Collects	£12,000
Charges	£510	Charges	£120
You receive	£16,490	You receive	£11,880
You write off	£3,510	You write off	£8,120

Some agencies work on a 'no collection-no charge basis' while others charge a nominal 'non-collection' fee.

Agencies vary too in the way the money they recover is paid to you. Some agencies encourage the debtor to pay you direct (they ask you to advise them as soon as they are paid). Other agencies ask the debtor to pay them (some ask for the cheque to be made out to the client) and account to you once a month or so. The former arrangement may appear preferable – money in the agency's account is no more use to you than money in the debtor's bank – but the latter arrangement allows the agency to retain control of the proceedings and to respond quickly if the cheque bounces, for instance.

Case Story 9

This company bought a pig in a poke

This cautionary tale illustrates the importance of deciding first what you want an agency to do for you, and how vital it is to read the small print.

A company (we'll call it XYZ Ltd) which dealt mainly with domestic customers and thus had many debts for small amounts of money, received a cold call from the representatives of a debt collection service. The rep's offer was, that for a fixed annual fee (based on turnover), the debt agency would undertake to collect any debts passed to it, and, if considered necessary, take court action against debtors with no extra cost

---

to XYZ (all the costs being covered by a special legal insurance included in the annual fee).

XYZ signed up, thinking this was one less thing to worry about (XYZ was surprised, though, to be asked to pay an enrolment fee of £100 as well as the annual subscription).

Six months later many debts still remained unpaid and XYZ asked the agency to take legal action. The agency refused to do so. It said the debts didn't qualify under the legal insurance scheme for one or more of the following reasons:

- XYZ hadn't obtained satisfactory creditworthiness references on the debtors before agreeing to grant credit (XYZ, remember, was dealing mainly with domestic customers where it's more difficult to make checks).
- Some debts were not submitted to the agency for collection within 45 days of falling due. (This is not very long and XYZ had been optimistic enough to think these customers would pay any day.)
- The legal insurance didn't cover debts of under £500 on which action could be taken through the Small Claims Court. (The agency did offer to do the paperwork on this for an extra fee, but it actually would have cost XYZ nothing except time to do it themselves.)
- The legal insurance didn't cover claims which were defended. These of course are the most difficult and expensive claims to pursue. With undefended claims, the plaintiff doesn't have to attend the hearing and can claim the costs back from the defendant.

Needless to say, the agency's rep hadn't mentioned any of these 'exclusions' to XYZ, but they were all written into the small print which XYZ hadn't bothered to read.

If XYZ had done so it would have realized that the legal insurance scheme was really of limited use to a company collecting debts for only small amounts from non-trade customers – it didn't provide the cover XYZ needed most.

Finding an agency

You need a firm with a thorough knowledge of the accountancy and legal aspects of debt collecting which will act with tact, skill and determination to achieve the maximum return for your business. Since the agency works for you, you need to be sure too that it works within the law. There are the odd rogues in the debt collection business who resort to aggressive tactics. It is, though, a criminal offence to 'harass' a debtor, threaten publicity or cause distress to the debtor or his family.

See first whether a colleague can recommend a reputable agency. If not check out those listed in *Yellow Pages* (under DEBT COLLECTORS), or contact the Credit Services Association (see Appendix A). This was formed as a controlling body for debt collecting firms and its members are required to comply with a Code of Practice and be covered by professional indemnity insurance. The CSA won't recommend a firm but will send you a list of its members.

Questions to ask

- Is the agency licensed for debt collection under the Consumer Credit Act 1974? A licence should be displayed on the premises.
- Are the principals members of any professional body, such as the Institute of Credit Management? It's not compulsory, but it should give you more reassurance if they are.
- How do they collect? By letter only? By letter and telephone? Personal visits? You might prefer your customers to be approached by some methods rather than others, and, anyway, you need to know what type of approach is going to be made to them.
- What's their performance record? It's useful to know what sort of success rate the agency anticipates and it helps you make more accurate cash calculations.
- What and how do they charge? If it's on commission see how much negotiation is possible in the rates (it's a very competitive industry). Are there any hidden charges? Do they charge a non-collection fee or not?
- How will the agency account to you for the monies collected? The quicker the better.
- How does the agency's legal collection service operate? Beware of agencies that use legal action to do their work for them. They may send a letter and sue simultaneously which bumps up your costs as a solicitor does the bulk of the work. Does the agency consult with clients before taking legal

action? What fees are charged to issue writs etc? What happens to costs recovered from debtors and interest on debts?

Statutory Demands for Payment

The Insolvency Act 1986 introduced a new method of extracting money from recalcitrant debtors. If the debt is for more than £750 and your requests for payment have been ignored, you can send your debtor a *Statutory Demand for Payment* form (see figure 14).

You buy these forms from law stationers, like Oyez. There are two separate forms, one to send to defaulting limited companies (reference 4.1) and another for individuals and non-incorporated firms – sole traders and partnerships (form 6.1).

A Statutory Demand is actually formally warning your debtor that one of its creditors (you) is alleging that the company/business is insolvent/bankrupt. The debtor has 21 days to respond. If he ignores the demand you are in theory entitled to file a petition for the compulsory winding-up of the business (if a limited company), or bankruptcy (if an individual or unincorporated firm).

Sending a Statutory Demand sounds rather extreme action to take but it can actually be both a very cheap (the forms cost around 50p) and a very effective way of getting your money quickly, since many debtors are not insolvent at all, just late-payers. And, by law, they have to react to the Demand. Company directors have a 'duty' to take timely action when financial difficulties loom (see Chapter 7). If the company has the cash, the sooner it pays the better.

Like writs and summonses, Statutory Demands have to be 'served' on the debtor. This means the Demand must be handed to the debtor, not posted. If your debtor really is in trouble, you need to decide whether you wish to proceed further and petition for winding-up or bankruptcy. This is more complicated and you may need a solicitor to help you do it. If you do petition, remember too that all creditors are equal so just because you are the petitioner doesn't mean your debt will be settled first.

A Statutory Demand for Payment is a powerful weapon, the receipt of which spells bad news for any business. It's probably sensible to use it judiciously; send it only when debts are undisputed and outstanding for some time – and when you are unlikely to want to do any further business with the debtor.

Figure 14 Statutory demand for payment form

Statutory Demand
under section 123(1)(a)
or 222(1)(a) of the
Insolvency Act 1986
No. 4.1* (Rule 4.5)

WARNING

- This is an **important** document. This demand must be dealt with **within 21 days** after its service upon the company or a winding-up order could be made in respect of the company.

- Please read the demand and notes carefully.

DEMAND

To

Address

This demand is served on you by the Creditor:

Name

Address

NOTES FOR CREDITOR

1. If the Creditor is entitled to the debt by way of assignment, details of the original Creditor and any intermediary assignees should be given in part B on page 3.

2. If the amount of debt includes interest not previously notified to the Company as included in its liability, details should be given, including the grounds upon which interest is charged. The amount of interest must be shown separately.

3. Any other charge accruing due from time to time may be claimed. The amount or rate of the charge must be identified and the grounds on which it is claimed must be stated.

4. In either case the amount claimed must be limited to that which has accrued due at the date of the demand.

5. If signatory of the demand is a solicitor or other agent of the Creditor, the name of his/her firm should be given.

The Creditor claims that the Company owes the sum of £   , full particulars of which are set out on page 2.

The Creditor demands that the Company do pay the above debt or secure or compound for it to the Creditor's satisfaction.

Signature of individual

Name
(BLOCK LETTERS)

Dated   19

*Position with or relationship to Creditor

*I am authorised to make this demand on the Creditor's behalf.

Address

Tel. No.   Ref No.

* Delete if signed by the Creditor himself.

N.B. The person making this Demand must complete the whole of this page, page 2 and parts A and B (as applicable) on page 3.

[P.T.O

*Reproduced by kind permission of the
Solicitors' Law Stationery Society Ltd*

7

Taking legal action

How to sue-it-yourself

Going to law should not necessarily be seen as a last resort, it's really just another method of galvanizing a lazy debtor to fork out your money, and you might prefer to use it as soon as your own collection efforts have failed rather than put old debts into the hands of a debt collection agency or send a Statutory Demand for Payment.

What's more, if you are in England and Wales it's now very easy to sue for debts of less than £1,000 in the county court. If the debt is not disputed you're unlikely to go anywhere near a court room, and if there is a hearing you don't need to be represented by a solicitor – it's not, in fact, in your interest to use one since you won't be allowed to claim the costs from the debtor.

This, though, might be a mixed blessing if you are so busy running your business that you prefer to offload problems of this nature onto the specialists. There may be a case here for employing the services of a debt collection agency and letting its lawyers, who are usually experienced in these matters, pursue the debt through the court for you.

You might anyway, before you sue, prefer to try the intermediate option of sending a solicitor's letter to your debtor – this is often enough to put the frighteners on.

However, since the purpose of this book is to ensure that you conserve your cash, forget about solicitors for the moment and read how to take your own case to court. This information only applies to England and Wales; there are no do-it-yourself facilities in the Sheriff Courts in Scotland or the District Court of Northern

Ireland. If you are based in England or Wales and need to sue through these courts it's best to instruct a solicitor in the area concerned rather than use an English or Welsh solicitor.

Debts up to £25,000 come under the jurisdiction of the county court. Claims for amounts above this figure *can* be heard in the county court but might be referred to the High Court. Undisputed claims for under £1,000 are normally dealt with by post, but where the debtor puts up a defence, claims are sorted out by *arbitration* rather than a full court hearing.

The purpose of arbitration is to enable people to have small disputes resolved in an informal atmosphere. The hearing takes place before an arbitrator, generally in private, without the formalities associated with a trial. No solicitors' costs are allowed save the costs shown on the summons, the costs of enforcing the judgment and costs incurred as a result of unreasonable conduct by a party in relation to the proceedings.

When the amount in dispute is above £1,000, the proceedings may also be referred to arbitration if both parties agree, but solicitors' costs *will* be allowed unless the parties in dispute ask for them to be excluded. There is nothing to stop you bringing a claim for more than £1,000 which goes to full trial without a solicitor, but if you lose and the other party has one, you might have to pay his costs.

Limited companies sometime find that the Registrar *does* direct them to be represented by a solicitor at an arbitration. Although the rules for the small claims procedure allow limited companies to be represented by an officer of the company or an authorized employee, this is at the discretion of the Registrar.

Who to sue

The importance of having the correct names and addresses for your customers was emphasized in Chapter 4, and it is particularly important if you are contemplating legal action.

If your debtor is a limited company, the summons has to be sent to its 'registered office' which is often a different address from the company's trading address. It should, however, be shown on the company's letterhead and/or invoice. If you don't know it you might be able to discover it from a company directory or a trade directory in your local reference library, otherwise you will have to get it from the Companies Registration Office.

At the time of writing it was possible to find out brief details of a company – its registration number, registered office, date last accounts were filed – for the price of a 'phone call to the Companies Registration Office in Cardiff or the London Search Room (see Appendix A for addresses) but it's likely that a charge will be introduced for telephone enquiries during 1991. You can call in person at the Cardiff and London offices to inspect the files and purchase a microfiche of them, costing £2.75. This can also be bought from the Companies Registration satellite offices in Leeds, Manchester, Birmingham, Glasgow and Edinburgh. The head office in Cardiff offers a postal service (a microfiche costs £5 and photocopies of company documents such as the last accounts, £6.50). If you prefer, you can employ a 'companies registration agent' (they are listed as such in *Yellow Pages*) to do a search for you (they will charge a fee of around £25).

If your debtor's business is a partnership, each partner is fully liable for the debts of the business. When you sue, it's sensible to name all the partners trading as such-and-such a firm at the address where the business is registered, as if you sue in the name of one partner only, and he/she doesn't pay, you can't then sue another.

You can't get blood out of a stone, so there is no point wasting time and money going to court if you know your debtor genuinely can't pay. You should think twice too if he is a perpetual defaulter. Find this out by checking the Registry of County Court Judgments. All judgments where £10 or more is outstanding one month after the date of the judgment, are registered, and remain on the register for six years. Anyone may call at the Registry Trust Ltd, or write asking for a search to be carried out (£2 at time of writing). If there is any suspicion that your debtor is already bankrupt, this can be checked at the Bankruptcy Search Room (address in Appendix A).

Find the court

You have two choices: the court of the area where the defendant lives or carries on business, or the court of the area where the 'events giving rise to the claim occurred'. Which court this is can sometimes be difficult to decide, especially where the contract was made by post. If, for instance, your debtor wrote to you out of the blue ordering some goods, the contract was made when you accepted his order. In which case the 'claim occurred' in the area of *your* county court. If, however, the debtor ordered the goods in response to your ad which contained the full purchase price, then the contract was made when the debtor posted the letter asking for them.

If you have chosen the wrong court, though, it is quite easy to get the action transferred. If you think you might have problems with your debtor, and may need to prise the money from him by resorting to one of the enforcement procedures mentioned later on, it could be sensible to elect for his local court at the outset since enforcement procedures have to be initiated in the debtor's local court.

Figure 15 Form for requesting issue of a default summons

Form for requesting issue of a default summons
- Please read the notes over the page before filling in this form. You will also find it useful to read the booklet "Small Claims in the County Court" which is available from any county court office.

For court use

Case number

Summons in form   N1 ☐
                   N2 ☐

Service by: Post ☐
           Plaintiff('s Solr) ☐

1 Plaintiff's
(Person making the claim)
Full name
Address

- Please be careful when filling in the request form.
- Type or write in block capitals using **black ink**.
- If the details of claim are on a separate sheet you must give the court a copy for its own use and a copy for each defendant.
- You can get help to complete this form at any county court office or citizens' advice bureau.

2 Plaintiff's solicitor
Address
Ref/tel no.

3 Defendant's
(Person against whom the claim is made)
Name
Address

4 What the claim is for
Give brief description of type of claim.

5 If the defendant does not live within the district of the court, the plaintiff states that the cause of action arose:

6 Particulars of the plaintiff's claim

7

Plaintiff's claim	
Court fee	
Solicitor's costs	
Total Amount	

For court use   Issued on

Small Claims Procedure
- Any defended claim for £500 or less will be automatically dealt with by arbitration. If you do not want the claim to be dealt with by arbitration you will have to apply to the court. The court office can give you more details.

9 If the claim exceeds £500 and you would like it to be dealt with by arbitration please tick the box below.

The claim exceeds £500 and I would like it to be dealt with by arbitration ☐

8 Signed
Plaintiff('s solicitor)
(or see attached form "Particulars of claim")

N 201   Request for default summons   Printed in the U.K. for H.M.S.O. 7/88 Dd8130651 C 4500 38806 G1835

Complete the forms

The forms you need are N201 'Form for requesting issue of a default summons' (see Figure 15); 'Certificate for Postal Service', and form N14 'Request for Entry of Judgment'.

Form N201 refers to you as the 'Plaintiff' and your debtor as the 'Defendant', and provides guidance notes on how to complete it. In the 'Particulars of Claim' box, you need to set out precise details of your claim (see Figure 16). If you wish to claim interest on the debt – and why not since this is allowed – you need to state this on the Particulars of Claim, specify the amount you can claim (currently 15 per cent) and calculate the amount of interest due to that date.

Figure 16 Specimen particulars of claim

IN THE . . . . . COUNTY COURT   CASE NO . . .
     BETWEEN   XYZ Ltd   Plaintiff
                      J. Smith & co   Defendant

(1) . . . . . 19 . . the Defendant agreed to purchase . . . . . (the goods) to the value of £. . . .
(2) The Plaintiff delivered the goods to the Defendant on . . . . . . but the Defendant has not paid for the goods.
(3) The Plaintiff claims £. . . . . as shown in the invoice numbered . . . . .
(4) The Plaintiff also claims interest under section 69 of the County Courts Act 1984 at the rate of . . . per cent per annum from . . . . (date) to . . . . (date) being £. . . . (total amount), and thereafter interest at the same rate up to the date of judgment.

Issue the summons

Take or post (send a s.a.e.) the completed form N201 and the signed Certificate for Postal Service to the court and pay the fee. At the time of writing the minimum court fee was £7; the maximum (for debts exceeding £500) £43.

The court will issue the summons and send you a 'Plaint Note' which confirms that the claim has been entered at court and shows the case number allocated to it. This is a vital document – make sure you keep it safe. The court files all cases by number, not name, so you need to quote the case number in any subsequent correspondence, and you will need to produce the Plaint Note in any dealings you have with the court, including further dealings like taking enforcement procedures. The court will post the summons to your debtor and will send you a note confirming the date of service.

Form N201 relates to a *Default* summons which is the type you need for recovering money. There is another type of summons called a *Fixed Date* summons which is issued when a claim is made for anything other than money – recovery of goods, possession of land etc.

In a default action no date is fixed for the parties to attend court. The debtor has 14 days to do one of the following: pay the debt plus the court fee; make an offer to pay weekly/monthly; enter a defence to the claim, or he might, of course, simply ignore the summons completely. If he does the latter, you are entitled to have judgment entered against him. You fill in form N14 and add in the interest from the date of the summons to the date of judgment and take it/send it with your Plaint Note.

If the debtor pays, the matter is at an end. Some shrewd debtors may, having received the summons, pay the debt but not the court fee. You can obtain judgment for that fee using N14 and enforce payment.

If the debtor offers payment by instalments you have the option to accept or reject the offer. If you accept, you then write to the court confirming this and they will order the debtor to pay on that basis. If you reject the offer, you contact the court and a date will be fixed for you and the debtor to attend a hearing where the court will decide how much the debtor must pay.

If a debtor delivers a defence, the court will send you a copy and, if the case is to be dealt with by arbitration, advise you of the hearing date. If the case is over the £1,000 limit the court will fix a date for a 'pre-trial' review. At that hearing the Registrar will consider the facts and direct what steps need to be taken to prepare the case for a full hearing.

Debtor's defence

Debtors can delay matters by delivering a defence, so you might receive a defence which you know has no real merit. In cases over £1,000 there's a way of dealing with phoney defences known as 'summary judgment procedure'. On receiving the defence you prepare an 'affidavit' – a short statement of the facts, when you deal with any points raised by the debtor. For example, the debtor might say: 'I did not receive the goods'. Your affidavit could then say: 'The goods were delivered to the defendant and I enclose copies of the signed delivery note'.

You have to swear on oath that the facts set out in the affidavit are correct, before a court official or a solicitor. The court will then fix a date as early as possible for a hearing. Both you and the debtor must attend and it is up to him to satisfy the court that he has a valid defence. If he can't, then judgment will be given against him. If he can, the case will go forward for hearing in the normal way.

Going to Court

If your case does go to court – either pre-trial review, arbitration or full trial – it is vital that you produce all the relevant documents – order forms, letters, invoices etc. The Registrar/Judge, after hearing the evidence from the parties in dispute, will usually deliver his judgment (it's called an award when the case goes to arbitration) there and then. If the case is complicated, though, or the Registrar/Judge wishes to consider any points of law, he might reserve his judgment in which case he will write to you later with his decision, if an arbitration case, or you will be sent a notice of another date to attend court when judgment will be given.

If you win the action, you can ask the court to order the defendant to pay your expenses in addition to the debt. If the case was heard by arbitration where no solicitors' costs are allowed, you can claim: any fees you paid to the court; any money you paid to witnesses (if you needed them); *your* expenses as a witness, ie the time you spent attending the hearing; out of pocket expenses such as the cost of plans, photographs used in evidence, fares, telephone calls, hotel bills if you had to spend the night away to attend the court, the cost of searching public registers such as the Companies Registration Office. In fact, any expenses incurred in preparing your case.

For more details of county court procedure, get *Small Claims in the County Court*, free from your local court office.

Case Story 10

Beware of clever debtors

Some debtors know how to play the legal system to their advantage and so delay payment as long as possible. To illustrate the ruses they adopt, here's the story of an architect who spent two years and three court hearings just to recover a straightforward debt.

The architect designed a house extension for a client. The client raised no objections so the architect sent in his bill for £907.

After eight months and despite several requests, no payment materialized so the architect handed the matter over to his solicitor. A summons was served and judgment was found in favour of the architect.

No money arrived. Four weeks later the architect's solicitors told him that the client had made an application for *Judgment to be set aside*. There are several grounds on which debtors can apply for judgment to be set aside, most commonly that the summons didn't reach the debtor (a default summons is served by post, unless personal service by bailiff is specifically requested), or that the debtor sent a defence which got lost.

The court believed the debtor and he was given leave to defend a re-hearing. He then produced a defence which the architect knew to be a tissue of lies. The re-hearing was scheduled for six months hence. However, just before the due date the client applied for the *hearing to be adjourned*. He'd found a technical hitch to slip through − he claimed he hadn't been sent a relevant document.

The hearing was re-scheduled for three months later but cancelled two days before when the client informed the architect's solicitor that he was prepared to *settle out of court*. The architect's jubilation was short-lived. No cheque arrived.

The case went back to court three months later. Neither the client nor his lawyer turned up and the Registrar concluded that 'there was no defence whatsoever' so the architect was awarded judgment plus interest plus costs.

Needless to say, the client didn't cough up within the 28 days limit and the bailiffs were sent in. Two months later the architect received his hard-won cash.

Enforcing the judgment: prising money from your debtor's hands

Getting judgment against your debtor is one thing, getting your hands on the money – alas – can be quite another.

There are several different procedures you can use to force the debtor to pay up if settlement isn't forthcoming in the time set by the court. The first three methods explained below don't require help from a solicitor – if you've successfully sued in the small claims court yourself, you don't want the expense of a solicitor now.

However, all these procedures take time to pursue and fees are involved, so, again, ask yourself whether the end result is going to be worth the effort. If you didn't check the Registry of County Court Judgments (see page 112) before you took the case to court, it might be sensible to check it now – the odds on a debtor with form paying your debt must be long.

What do you know about your debtor? If a limited company is it still trading? Does it have property/assets? If an individual or the owner of a partnership or sole trader, does he/she have a house? car? other assets?

If you don't know very much about your debtor, which is very common, the court offers a useful intermediate step prior to taking one of the enforcement procedures detailed below: you can apply to have your debtor examined on oath as to his ability to pay the debt.

This is known as an 'Oral Examination', and it's not in the debtor's interest to try to avoid it since if he fails to attend he can be sent to prison for contempt of court.

Oral Examination: discover his means

Although an Oral Examination won't itself result in retrieving your cash, it should give you some indication as to which of the enforcement methods is most likely to succeed – or whether it's better to forget the whole thing.

To organize an Oral Examination you go to the county court where the debtor lives or carries on business (usually this will be the court where you obtained judgment; if not, you need to write to the Registrar of that court and ask for the proceedings to be transferred), and pick up form N316 from the court office.

When you return the completed form with your fee, the court

issues an order to the debtor requiring him to attend and to bring with him any documents relating to his finances, and lets you know the date.

As you are the one meant to be asking the questions you should go in person. If, however, you can't attend or are nervous about quizzing your debtor, the Registrar will do it for you and, on payment of a fee, will give you a written note of the debtor's answers which the debtor is required to sign.

If the debtor is a limited company, you may examine a director, the company secretary or any other officer of the firm (get their names from the Companies Registry) if you don't already know them, or they don't appear on the letterhead. Your questions here can only relate to the property of the company itself, eg what assets are possessed by the firm; the whereabouts of these assets, not the director's/officer's private assets. Where your debtor is in partnership, a sole trader or an individual, you can ask about both their business and personal assets. Here's a guide to the sort of questions you need answers to:

- Whether they own their own house/flat; if so is it in the debtor's name only or jointly with the spouse; when it was bought; the title number at the Land Registry; present value; how much owing on mortgage; monthly mortgage payments. If rented, how much is paid per month.
- Which bank and building society accounts are held and where; account numbers and current balance in each.
- Details of premium bonds, stocks and shares.
- Whether the debtor owns a motor vehicle; its make and registration; whether paid for or on HP or credit sale; present value; if on HP, monthly repayments and how much is still owing.
- Whether the debtor owns furniture, TV, video etc; whether any items are on HP and, if so, which items and how much is owed.
- Details of any other property owned.
- If he has children, their ages.
- Whether he has any other debts; court orders against him.

If the debtor is an individual, find out also:

- Name and address of employer; works number or pay

reference number.

- Basic pay; average take-home pay including overtime; any other earnings.
- Whether spouse has a job and if so what he/she earns.

Ask too if the debtor is prepared to make an offer of payment at the end of the Oral Examination. If he does and it's acceptable you can ask the court to make a new order there and then and the whole business will be finished with.

If the debtor fails to attend the first hearing, he does, in fact, get a second chance, and this time he comes up before a judge who can commit him to prison if he refuses to be examined (or doesn't turn up). For this hearing he can ask you for his travelling expenses to and from the court. These will be added to the money he already owes you. You can't refuse to supply this 'conduct' money if asked for, otherwise if the debtor fails to attend the hearing the judge may be unable to send him to prison. It's important to note that you have to write to the court no earlier than four days before the hearing, stating either that the debtor has not asked you for conduct money or that you have paid him a reasonable amount for travelling expenses.

Warrant of Execution: send in the bailiff

This is not as drastic as it sounds, nor as severe as you may have hoped. It simply means the court bailiff goes to the debtor's home or business premises and, if the debtor won't pay him the money that you are owed, removes and sells sufficient of the debtor's goods to satisfy your debt and the costs of the sale.

To start the ball rolling you produce your Plaint Note (see page 114) at the court office, fill in form N323 and pay the fee – which varies according to the amount for which the warrant is to be issued.

The bailiff goes round (he cannot force entry into a debtor's house, but he can, if necessary, to business premises), inspects the goods and selects those which he thinks will raise enough at auction to pay the debt as well as the costs involved in their removal and sale.

Quite often, unfortunately, you will receive a report from the court that there are insufficient goods. This is especially infuriating if you know your debtor lives in the lap of luxury! But there might be good reaons: the bailiff can't seize just anything. He must allow the debtor to keep clothes and bedding to the value of £100, and the tools and implements of his trade up to the value of £150. He can't take anything that's owned by the debtor's wife or landlord or anything on hire purchase – and that's often the most valuable stuff: cars, videos, washing machines etc. Also, goods fetch very little at public auctions and the costs of removal and sale are fairly substantial.

If you know your debtor owns a car or other expensive items, tell the bailiff when you issue the warrant – and at the same time make sure the debtor hasn't moved house.

The debtor may agree to sign a 'walking possession' agreement which allows him to retain the goods, but if he doesn't raise the money pronto the bailiff can re-enter the premises (this time he can use force) and remove the goods.

A warrant remains in force for a year so if you discover during that time that the debtor does have goods worth taking, you can ask for the warrant to be re-issued.

Attachment of Earnings order: ask the debtor's employer to pay you

The court makes an order directing the debtor's employers to deduct a set amount from the debtor's wages each week/month and pay it to you. This enforcement procedure can only be used if the debtor is an individual and employed. It's no good if your debtor is a limited company, a partner in a firm or self-employed.

Before you go ahead, it's a good idea to discover whether anyone else has an Attachment of Earnings order against the debtor. The court maintains an index which they will search for you. If there are other orders the debtor might not earn enough to pay yours as well as others; if you decide to go ahead, it will probably be postponed until the others are paid off.

You take your Plaint Note to the court in the area where the debtor lives (again, you will have to have your case transferred if this is not the court where you obtained judgment), fill in form N337 and pay the fee. You will be told when the application is to be heard (you can, if you wish, ask the court to proceed in your absence).

It might not actually get as far as a hearing, though. The debtor might complete the form he has been sent and make an offer to pay what he thinks he can afford. If the court receives this in good time, it will make a provisional order and send it to you. If you approve, the order will be made and sent to the employer.

Garnishee proceedings: get your money straight out of your debtor's bank

If someone owes money to your debtor you can ask the court to order that person (called the garnishee) to pay the money you are owed to the court which then pays it to you – so long as the debt is for £25 or more.

How do you find out who your debtor has financial dealings with? Most of the time you don't need to know, because money held by a bank is a debt due by the bank to its customer, so you 'garnish' the debtor's bank or building society.

An important point to note here: a garnishee order only applies to money which is in the account on the date the order is served – not to money which is paid in later. So if the account is overdrawn on that day, you won't get anything. If your debtor is an individual rather than a business think carefully about the timing of your application; people who are paid a monthly salary, for instance, are more likely to be richer at the beginning of the month than at the end.

You need to know the name and address of the debtor's bank/building society (this is where an oral examination mentioned above can be so helpful). If you just know the name of the bank, you can still make an order but it might take the bank some time to find the right account and by that time the debtor may have withdrawn his money!

When you have filled in form N349 (which you obtain from the court office) you have to swear on oath that the information you have given is true. You can do this before a court official or a solicitor.

The Registrar will consider your application without you or the debtor present. If satisfied, he will make an interim order (a garnishee order nisi) which is sent to the garnishee and the debtor. Unless either of them can put up a decent argument, the garnishee order is made absolute. It should be said that a bank won't act as garnishee for love, it will charge clerical expenses – up to around £30 – and these are deducted first so if there isn't sufficient money in the debtor's account to cover both your debt and the expenses you will only get the balance.

If the bank claims there is no money in the debtor's account, or not enough, and you don't believe this or have reason to think the debtor has another account with the bank, then the court will hold a hearing.

Charging orders: sell his house

If your debtor has assets – a house, for example, or shares in a company – then, if you have a judgment against him you can apply for a 'Charging Order'. If granted, this gives you a 'charge' – a form of mortgage – over that asset.

If the charge is for land that is registered, you can register the order with the Land Registry without the consent of the debtor.

This might frighten the debtor enough to pay up. If it doesn't – or he can't – you need to make another application to the court for leave to sell the house or whatever.

You then sell the asset for the best possible price; pay off any other mortgages (if a property) – prior charges such as first and second mortgages take priority over your debt; take what is owed to you, plus the cost of the sale, and pay any balance remaining back to the debtor.

As you can see, this is a far more complicated way of enforcing a judgment and not recommended without help from a solicitor, or unless you are pretty sure the end result will be worthwhile.

Finally, you can go straight for the jugular and try to extract your cash by petitioning for *winding up* a limited company, or *bankrupting* an individual or unincorporated business. And you can do this without having been through the court and getting judgment by using a Statutory Demand for payment (see last chapter) so it is potentially a much quicker solution than the enforcement procedures described above.

What to do if your customer goes bust

There is a terrible temptation just to grin and bear it when a debtor goes into liquidation or bankruptcy. Resist it – there might well be something to salvage.

The Insolvency Act 1986 radically changed the law relating to company insolvency and individual bankruptcy, which is good news for creditors, but less good news for directors of limited liability companies who now need to keep a close watch on their company's financial state. If they don't, and it goes bust, they may be disqualified from being a director of any company for two years and could even lose the protection of limited liability and be made *personally* liable for the company's debts.

Company insolvency

If a company gets into financial difficulties, it has the following options:

1 To put forward a plan to creditors, explaining the difficulties it faces and outlining its proposals for resolving them.
2 To ask the court to make an Administration Order to formalize a scheme with its creditors.
3 To ask a debenture holder – ie a bank which has lent it money under a legal charge over company assets – to appoint a Receiver to manage its affairs.
4 To call a meeting of creditors and go into Creditors Voluntary Liquidation.

What a company in financial trouble should not do is sit back and hope the problem goes away. This is a breach of the Insolvency Act and allows creditors to press for compulsory winding-up. If the company becomes insolvent and it can be shown that any director, as a result of his or her conduct, is unfit to be concerned in the management of a company, that person can be disqualified by the courts. And if the courts are satisfied that before the actual insolvency the director(s) knew, or ought to have known, that there was no reasonable prospect of avoiding insolvency, but allowed the company to continue trading, the courts might find the director(s) guilty of the offence of 'wrongful trading' and order them to pay some contribution to creditors.

The different options

If your debtor company takes the first of the options outlined above, it is important to consider the company's proposals carefully, and perhaps take professional advice, since whether they work or not has a material effect on creditors.

Option two is not very common but it could be very much to the creditors' advantage. It means the directors of the company (or its creditors) apply to the court to have an 'Administrator' (a qualified insolvency practitioner) take over the day-to-day running of the business with a view to making it viable again. The administrator has three months to put forward a rescue plan, and a meeting of creditors will be held within the three-month period to vote on whether to accept or reject the administrator's proposals. Again, study them carefully. Over half of the albeit small number of firms which have appointed administrators to date *have* returned to the corporate fold in one form or another and are making profits.

Protection is what an Administration Order provides – protection of the company's assets while the administrator has the opportunity of assessing its potential. This means no creditor can take legal action against the company; no creditor who has supplied goods on lease, rental or HP may take the goods back; no creditor who has supplied goods subject to 'retention of title' (see page 128) may claim them. If the administrator fails, liquidation is likely to follow.

Receivers (option three) also take over the day-to-day running of a troubled company but they see their task as selling as many of the company's assets as necessary to pay off the debts for the debenture holder or creditor who appointed them, so the protection mentioned above does not apply.

If the company goes into voluntary or compulsory liquidation, it's still worth going to the meeting of creditors or getting someone to represent you – there might be more money available than you think.

Creditors' meeting

As a creditor you will receive a notice of a Meeting of Creditors, a Statement of Affairs which sets out the assets and liabilities of the company, and a Form of Proxy which enables you to appoint someone to attend the meeting and vote, on your behalf, for a liquidator (a qualified insolvency practitioner) who ensures the assets are properly protected and realized for the benefit of the creditors.

The meeting, grisly though it probably will be, is an opportunity to ask questions relating to the company's Statement of Affairs. Has the financial position of the company changed significantly since you decided to grant credit? If so, for what reason? When did the directors of the company realize it was insolvent? What was the cause of the insolvency? Scrutinize the figures presented carefully – one company's Statement of Affairs contained a figure of £10,000 for 'wages, salaries and holiday pay' which on close questioning turned out to be a bonus voted to the MD six months earlier for his 'unstinting efforts which have resulted in substantial orders which will ensure the continuing profitability of the company'!

With the Statement of Affairs you will also receive a list of fellow creditors. The debtor is going to be 'investigated' under the Insolvency Act. If the investigation is going to be thorough, it's up to the creditors to make it so. What do you know about the debtor? What do other creditors know? Sharing information and getting together to present a united front often pays dividends – real dividends in cash.

Should you be unable/unwilling to go to the meeting, you can appoint a qualified insolvency practitioner to go in your place, using your Form of Proxy. He won't charge you anything, and he will know exactly what questions need asking. This is where it's really sensible to band together with other creditors and get the same person to act for all of you. The Department of Trade and Industry publishes a list of qualified insolvency practitioners (available from HMSO shops), but most of the large accountancy firms: Coopers & Lybrand, Deloitte, Ernst and Young, Peat Marwick McLintock, Price Waterhouse, for example, offer this service. Telephone (they all have London offices) and ask to speak to the Insolvency Co-ordinator or someone who can help regarding creditors' meetings.

When it comes to sharing out whatever money remains, be aware that all creditors are equal but some are more equal than others. Wages and salaries due to staff, money owed to the Inland Revenue, Customs and Excise and the debtor's bank will be paid first. 'Unsecured creditors' such as trade creditors like yourself share whatever is left – if anything. If nothing, you have the small consolation of being able to claim back the VAT.

Bankruptcy

If your debtor is an individual or unincorporated business (ie a sole trader or partnership), petitioning for bankruptcy is the only option open to you if you've taken him/her to court and tried to enforce the judgement without success, and/or sent a Statutory Demand for Payment (see last chapter) which has been ignored for at least 21 days.

An individual or unincorporated business in financial trouble, but with some assets, may first attempt to avert bankruptcy by applying to the court to make a 'Voluntary arrangement' as to how the debts will be paid off. Voluntary arrangements are formal procedures supervised by an insolvency practitioner, and the insolvency practitioner advising the debtor will also apply for an interim order to prevent creditors from taking further legal action to enforce repayment of debts and to stop them taking court action to make the debtor bankrupt.

The voluntary arrangement will come into effect only if the creditors approve the debtor's proposals. If agreement is reached, the insolvency practitioner will supervise the debtor's affairs and decide how debts will be paid. If any creditor wants to change any of the decisions of the insolvency practitioner they must apply to the court.

The debtor can still be made bankrupt if he:

- Fails to comply with his obligations.
- Provides misleading information.
- Fails to do what the insolvency practitioner reasonably requires.

A voluntary arrangement will usually be better for creditors than bankruptcy since the business should continue to produce profits for their benefit.

If your debtor has a county court judgment against him and his total debts don't exceed £5,000 the court may agree to make an *Administration Order* which enables the debtor to pay a fixed amount every month into the court which distributes the money to the creditors named in the Order on a pro rata basis.

When an application for an Administration Order is filed, the court will notify the creditors with a date for a hearing. Creditors are entitled to exclude themselves from Administration Orders but it is usually only practicable to do so if there is a quicker remedy available for the recovery of the debt – the legal right to repossess goods bought on hire purchase, for example.

If your debtor has no money at all, he may well react to your Statutory Demand by applying to the court to make himself bankrupt (which saves you the fee). If he doesn't do this and doesn't apply for a voluntary arrangement, or come to any agreement with you, or apply to have the demand set aside (within 18 days of receiving the Statutory Demand), there is nothing for it but to apply to the court to make him bankrupt on a form called a 'creditor's petition' (you can band together with other creditors to do this).

You need to show that your debtor has failed to comply with a Statutory Demand for the debt, or failed to comply with a voluntary arrangement or that you have a court order for debt against the debtor which you have tried unsuccessfully to enforce.

When the court hears the creditor's petition it won't necessarily make the debtor bankrupt, unless there is no way the debtor can pay his debts by instalments or otherwise. If the debtor is adjudicated bankrupt, his business and his assets will pass into the hands of the Official Receiver who will sell off the assets to pay the creditors. And, as with creditors of limited companies, secured and preferential creditors, eg the debtor's bank and the Inland Revenue, will get paid first.

Retention clauses

If you've delivered goods on credit and your buyer goes broke before paying for them, you stand to lose out twofold – no money and no goods to resell. The way to make sure the goods remain yours by law until full payment has been made is to insert a clause in your Terms and Conditions of Sale (see page 93).

This should say something like:

Title to Goods

Risk in the goods passes to the buyer on delivery but title remains vested in the Company so long as any sum due to the Company, on whatever account or grounds, is unpaid. The buyer agrees that the Company in seeking to exercise its rights under this clause may at any reasonable time enter the buyer's premises and remove the Company's goods.

The wording of the clause needs to be carefully drafted and it is sensible to enlist the help of a solicitor. It has to be said that these "retention of title" clauses, as they are called, have been the subject of much debate in the courts and some firms have not been able to rely on them when disaster strikes.

For the clause to have a chance of working:

- You must be able to prove that the customer knew and accepted your terms of business. Your retention clause must therefore be set out in your quotation or terms of sale, or brought to the customer's attention in your price list or in a letter sent before the deal is concluded.

- Your products must be clearly identifiable (bearing your trademark or packed in packaging which carries your name). If you supply a standard product which can't be distinguished from that of other suppliers, the clause may not help you.
- You must be able to link the particular goods to the unpaid invoices.

One point to bear in mind. If you do claim retention of title, you can't claim VAT bad-debt relief.

8

Trading abroad

Exporting is undoubtedly a more hazardous business than selling to the domestic market, yet, ironically, getting paid for overseas sales is often quicker and more certain than for home sales.

Because of the potentially horrendous cash flow problems created for exporters by the lengthy interval likely to occur between placing the order and payment of same, methods of payment for exporting have evolved which allow exporters to receive payment much earlier than they would if payment was left solely to the buyer.

These methods involve the banks, and they are activated when documents relating to the sale are placed with the bank (see *Documentary letters of credit* on page 133 and *Bills of exchange* on page 136. The money is often guaranteed by the bank too, and/or covered by insurance (much more common in exporting than in domestic transactions). In theory, therefore, the exporter has less worry over bad debts, less need of sophisticated credit control procedures, and should find it much easier to do cash flow forecasts.

Minimizing the risks

However, it's not necessarily all plain sailing. Many exporting firms find their buyers are unwilling to agree to documentary collection methods of payment, and exporting firms that do use them won't get paid promptly unless the documentation is one hundred per cent correct – and there are an awful lot of documents to get right when exporting.

Thus it's essential that firms involved in exporting have

adequate working capital to cover the additional costs likely to be incurred (see page 132), and to cope with the cash flow problems which can be caused by long payment delays.

Firms with an established record and increasing export prospects, but constrained by problems of raising finance, often find export factoring the right solution. The factor advances somewhere between 70–80 per cent of the exporter's outstanding debts and takes over the exporter's sales ledger and credit collection procedures in return for a fee based on turnover (factoring is explained in detail in the next chapter).

It is also possible to raise a loan for exporting on an insurance policy from the Export Credits Guarantee Department. The ECGD was set up as a government department in 1919 to help British exporters insure against the risks of selling overseas (ECGD Insurance Services are to be privatized during 1991). ECGD insurance policies protect against *buyer* risks and *country* risks. Unlike domestic credit insurance, cover against buyer risks is not limited to the buyer becoming insolvent; it also includes the buyer's failure to pay within six months after the due date for goods accepted, and the buyer's failure or refusal to accept despatched goods which comply with the contract.

Country risk cover protects against the contract not being performed, or payment not being received, due to political, economic and other factors. You are normally covered for 90 per cent of loss in cases of the buyer's default or insolvency, and 95 per cent for the country risk. Cover normally starts on the date of shipment although certain exporters can get cover from the date of contract on payment of a higher premium. Premiums depend on what cover is being provided for which countries. All sorts of specialized export insurance is also available from ECGD.

Regarding loan facilities, ECGD, as an extension of its insurance services, provides direct guarantees to banks. The security of such guarantees means the banks are prepared to provide finance to the exporter so that he receives the majority of the cash for the sale at, or very shortly after, shipment of the goods or performance of contracted work. This finance is frequently provided at preferential fixed rates of interest because of ECGD's intervention.

You don't necessarily need to deal direct with ECGD to raise money, though. Many intermediaries, notably the big banks, operate schemes whereby a number of businesses are covered by a master ECGD policy. This offers a combination of export finance and credit insurance at cheaper administrative costs. Some intermediaries link the policy with an invoice discounting service (see Chapter 9), and to credit management and debt collection services.

Credit status reports (see Chapter 4) need to be taken out on new overseas customers, especially if payment is on normal, open account terms. As well as the specialized credit reference agencies, these can be obtained through the Government's British Overseas Trade Board, and all the big banks can supply them via their overseas correspondent banks.

Costs and trading terms

When a product is sold overseas, there are usually far more costs to be recovered before there can be any profit. Apart from the costs of producing the goods, the additional costs you may or may not have to pay when exporting include: export packing; inland transport and handling to port; export transport; insurance; handling and transport costs overseas; any taxes, customs duties payable overseas including VAT, sales and/or purchase taxes; freight forwarders' charges; overseas agents' charges; cost of foreign money exchange and credit, and cost of cover against exchange rate risks, if applicable.

Which of these costs are involved will depend to some extent on how you do business, and will also depend on the terms of the contract you make with your buyer. Apart from stating the agreed type, quality, quantity and price of the goods, mode of payment and delivery date, the contract must stipulate which items are included in the price, and who will be responsible for arranging and paying for transport and insurance.

In international trade this is done with a range of abbreviations, known as 'incoterms'. (The International Chamber of Commerce – see Appendix A – publishes a *Guide to Incoterms* which contains the full list.) Here are the most common incoterms which indicate which charges are covered by the selling price:

- **Ex-Works**: the buyer takes delivery and possession of the goods at your factory gate and is responsible for all further charges.

- **FOT** (Free on truck): the exporter undertakes to load the goods onto the collection vehicle and bear the cost of loading.
- **FAS** (Free alongside Ship): the exporter delivers the goods alongside the nominated delivery vessel and pays all charges to that point.
- **FOB** (Free on Board): the exporter is responsible for all costs until the goods are loaded on to the carrying vessel. The exporter is not responsible for the sea-freight or marine insurance.
- **C & F (Cost and Freight)**: the contract price includes freight charges to the named port of destination, but not insurance.
- **CIF (Cost, Insurance, Freight)**: this includes all costs, including insurance, until the goods are unloaded at the port of discharge.
- **DDP (Delivery Duty Paid)**: this covers all the costs of delivery to the buyer's premises, including any duty payable.

When shown on invoices and other documentation these payment terms should always be expressed so that they show the point of delivery, where responsibility for the goods passes to the buyer, eg 'FOB Liverpool', 'CIF New York', 'DDP Buyer's warehouse, Milan'.

Methods of payment

Advance payment

Nice if you can get it, and wonderful for your cash flow! But it's very rare that a buyer will wish to extend credit to the supplier with the added risk that the goods will not arrive, be delayed or arrive in an unsatisfactory condition. Other than where a supplier sells a rare product and can thus dictate terms, cash with order is only common for small sample orders and in mail-order business.

Documentary letters of credit

A letter of credit is a written undertaking from a bank that it will pay the exporter provided the exporter produces documentry evidence that the goods have been shipped and that all the terms and conditions laid down in the letter of credit have been complied with.

Figure 17 Documentary letter of credit

United World Chinese Commercial Bank

KAOHSIUNG BRANCH
245 Chung Cheng 4th Road
Kaohsiung, Taiwan, Republic of China

TELEX: 72138
CABLE: "UWCBANK"
TEL: (07) 2711140-9
FAX: (07) 2716824

☐ CONFIRMATION OF TELEX/CABLE PRE-ADVISED   Date: Nov. 2. 1988

IRREVOCABLE DOCUMENTARY CREDIT	Credit No.	Expiry Date For Negotiation
Advising Bank	8FK2/0709	Mar. 10. 1989

The Bank of California NA London   REF : E90-6166

Beneficiary
Weir Engineers Ltd Unit 4 Station Ind.Est. Fleet Hants CU 138QY England

Applicant
Taiwan Machinery Mfg Corp No. 3 Tai-Chi Rd Hsiao Kang Kaohsiung Taiwan

Amount
STG6,629.00 POUND STERLING SIX THOUSAND SIX HUNDRED TWENTY NINE ONLY

Dear Sirs,
We hereby issue in your favor this Documentary Credit whith is available by negotiation of your draft
at ------ sight for invoice value drawn on us
bearing the number of this Credit and out name accompanied by the following documents (disregard items not marked in ☐)

6 ☐ Signed Commercial Invoices, indicating Import Permit No. 77KA1-003761
☐ Full ☒ ½ set of clean on board ocean Bills of Lading made out to order of UNITED WORLD CHINESE COMMERCIAL BANK marked "Freight
☐ Clean Air Waybills consigned to us marked "Freight
☐ Prepaid/ ☐ Collect" and notify the applicant indicating this L/C number.
☐ Insurance policy or Certificate in duplicate, endorsed in blank for 110% invoice value in currency of draft covering Institute
  Cargo Clauses (☐ A ☐ B ☐ C ☐ AIR) ☐ Institute War Clauses (☐ Cargo/ ☐ Air Cargo)
    ☐ All Risks ☐ W.A. ☐ F.P.A.
  ☐ Institute Strikes Clauses (☐ Cargo/ ☐ Air Cargo) ☐ Institute Theft Pilferage and Non-Delivery (insured value) Clauses
  Claim if any, payable in Taiwan
☒ Supplier's Certificate (required only on shipment involving payment of agent commission, to be filled in the form as printed
  on the reverse).
☒ Beneficiary's Certificate stating that a duplicate set of shipping documents required herein
  including a negotiable Bill of Lading has been forwarded direct to the applicant by registered airmail.
4 has accompanied shipment
4 Packing Lists.
x Inspection Certificate in Triplicate issued by Maker

Covering
** 4. For negotiation with discrepancy direct reimbursement claim to reimbursing bank is
      subject to issuing bank's authorization

Covering:
48 sets of 38 Valve Group
(Details as per Contract No. TMMC-77146 Dated Oct 19 1988)   ALL CHARGES OUTSIDE TAIWAN SUCH AS ADVISING/NEGOTIATION/REIMBURSEMENT COMMISSION/
☒ FOB / ☐ C&F / ☐ CIF / ☐   POSTAGE AND STAMP DUTY ETC. ARE FOR ACCOUNT OF BENEFICIARY
Free European Port

Shipment from	to	Latest	Partial Shipments	Transhipment
Free European Port	Kaohsiung Port	Feb. 28. 1989	not Allowed	not Allowed

SPECIAL CONDITIONS. 1. Shipment must be effected through Schenker & Co GmbH and/or their Affiliated Company
2. If cargo is Shipped later than shipment date the beneficiary has to pay delay penalty
   on the basis of 0.1% of the invoice value for each day's delay. Such penalty should be
   deducted from the negotiating amount by the negotiating bank
3. B/L dated within 30 days after the shipment date specified above is acceptable. Under
   such circumstances the validity of the credit is proportionally extended.
   NEGOTIATION IS RESTRICTED TO THE (FIRST) ADVISING BANK ☐ SIMPLE RECEIPT INSTEAD OF DRAFT ACCEPTABLE.

FOR REIMBURSEMENT: The negotiating bank is requested to ☐ telex us of the negotiated amount
                            and certify to this effect on the covering schedule then
x ☐ draw sight draft on/ ☐ debit our Head office account with/ ☐ claim on American Express Bank Ltd London
  claim on us by designating a depository bank in New York, we shall reimburse by airmail upon receipt of documents.
  ☐ at maturity of draft, we shall cover negotiating bank as designated
for the face amount of draft negotiated, referring to the Credit number, (which implies that all terms and conditions of this
Credit have been complied with.)

We hereby engage to pay drawers and/or bona fide holders that drafts drawn and negotiated
in conformity with the terms of this credit will be duly honoured on presentation and
drafts accepted within the terms of this credit will be duly honoured at maturity
The amount of each draft must be endorsed on the reverse of this Credit by the
negotiating bank. All documents are to be despatched to us
  in one airmail | X in two by consecutive airmails
                Yours faithfully,
      UNITED WORLD CHINESE COMMERCIAL BANK
              KAOHSIUNG BRANCH

SIGNATURE
VERIFIED BY

Advising bank's notification & ref. number

We advise this Credit without engagement
on our part.

Authorised Signatory,
Bank of California, London 9th November 1988
Date. stamp and signature of advising bank

(1 1-008, 77. 7)   1 ORIGINAL

Letters of credit are a means of effecting payment, not financial instruments like bills of exchange (these may be the mechanism under which payment is made on a letter of credit, but it's possible for payment to be made without them). Letters of credit are the most secure way of being paid for exported goods but buyers are sometimes reluctant to agree to them as a means of payment since the commitment made on the buyer's behalf by his bank will form part of his banking facilities. Also, bank charges for letters of credit are not cheap.

There are 'unconfirmed' and 'confirmed' letters of credit. An unconfirmed letter of credit is a commitment from the buyer's bank to pay the exporter once it is satisfied everything is in order. Since the bank should not agree to accept this risk unless it is sure that the customer has the necessary funds, this should be a safe enough bet. And most times it is, but there have been cases where overseas banks have put companies out of business by refusing to honour unconfirmed letters of credit.

You get complete protection with a 'confirmed' letter of credit. This means that your buyer's bank arranges for the debt to by paid by a bank in the UK. Payment is thus guaranteed, provided you comply with the terms of the letter of credit. There is no risk of non-payment even if the buyer defaults or goes broke, or for any outside reason such as the imposition of exchange control restrictions.

Here's how letters of credit work: at the instigation of the buyer, his bank opens a letter of credit in favour of the exporter. This bank, known as the 'issuing bank', contacts a bank in the country where the seller trades and this bank (the advisory bank) sends the exporter a copy of the letter of credit, and perhaps agrees to confirm the letter if this is requested.

Now the exporter can fulfil the order and despatch the goods, at the same time forwarding all the documentation to the advisory bank. If the documents are found to be in order, the advisory bank then credits the exporter's account with payment.

Next, the advisory bank sends the documents to the issuing bank which checks them in its turn and re-imburses the paying bank. The issuing bank will then release the documents to the buyer on payment of the amount due, or on previously agreed terms.

Sounds simple enough, but letters of credit are actually very complex documents, as are the procedures which accompany them. The documentation you submit must comply precisely with every detail stipulated in the letter of credit – a single mistake in a document, or any point of non-compliance means the bank *has* to refuse payment.

Letters of credit themselves can take time to get right. A survey carried out a few years ago found that 49 per cent of letters of credit presented to the banks were unacceptable when first seen. Often the problem is just a typing error – it took one engineering firm, though, three months to sort out a letter of credit where the buyer firm had typed '½ VALUE' instead of '½" VALVE'! The banks charge quite heavily for changing letters of credit too. Letters of credit can be 'revocable' or 'irrevocable (they should state which). In practice you are only likely to come across irrevocable letters of credit which means that no alterations can be made without prior agreement of buyer and exporter.

Bills of exchange

Bills of exchange can be used on their own, without letters of credit, to get payment on production of documentation. A bill of exchange is a legal instrument. Rather like a post-dated cheque, it is drawn by the exporter on his buyer, directing him to pay a set amount on a certain date. This is the legal definition given in the Bills of Exchange Act 1882:

- An unconditional order in writing, addressed by one person to another, signed by the person giving it, requiring the person to whom it is addressed to pay on demand or at a fixed or determinable future time a sum certain in money or to the order of a specified person or to bearer.

The bill of exchange is handed to your bank together with the other documentation relating to the particular sale. Your bank sends the bills and other documents to the appropriate overseas bank, which notifies your buyer of their arrival. The bank will then 'release' the documents to your buyer which enables him to take delivery of the goods.

If the bill of exchange is drawn 'at sight', your buyer must first pay the full amount shown on the bill. If you are extending credit, the bill will be drawn for payment a number of days 'after sight'; or on some specified future date. In this case, the buyer signs the bill to show that he has accepted it, and contracts to pay the full amount on the due date.

Although there is no guarantee of payment as with confirmed letters of credit, legal procedures exist in many countries to recover money against accepted bills of exchange. (More on bills of exchange in Chapter 9.)

Figure 18   Bill of Exchange

Sight bill of exchange.

No. 120

Exchange *for* £2,560   BT&. *b.s.t* 19*&s*

AT SIGHT   *of this* FIRST BILL *of Exchange*

/   SECOND   *of the same tenor and date being unpaid/pay to the*

order of OURSELVES   *the sum of*

TWO THOUSAND FIVE HUNDRED AND SIXTY POUNDS ONLY

To ADAM STEVENS LTD

NEW YORK   USA

FOR AND ON BEHALF OF
J D P CLOTHING LTD

DIRECTOR

Open account

This is the straightforward payment after receipt of goods, on normal credit terms, used in domestic sales. It is the least secure way of doing business abroad unless you have complete confidence in the integrity of your buyer. However, many importers in Europe and the USA won't trade on any other terms so it is a very common method of doing business, particularly when firms have become well-established trading partners and are familiar with each other's procedures.

If the buyer pays you by cheque or international money order, it can be an age before you get paid, though. The cheque could be in the post for as long as a month and then be delayed passing through the international banking system. There will be further delays if exchange control authority has first to be obtained in the importer's country.

To speed things up the seller may be able to arrange with his bank for the cheque to be 'negotiated/purchased with recourse'. The bank will then make funds available before the cheque has been finally cleared in the buyer's country (the bank will retain the right to charge back the customer's account should the cheque be unpaid). And the bank will, of course, charge interest for the service.

Payment by *banker's draft*, whereby the purchaser arranges for his bank to issue a draft on a UK bank in either sterling or a foreign currency won't cut out delays in the post but it does mean the draft will be cleared quickly once it arrives, and, in theory, it is a more secure form of payment.

Payment by *International Money Transfer* is a much quicker way to get paid and results in the exporter receiving cleared funds direct into his bank account. The importer first instructs his bank to make payment through the banking system (the exporter must be sure to indicate his account number and bank branch on his invoice if this is the chosen method of payment). The buyer's bank then instructs a bank in the seller's country to make the payment. This instruction can be sent by mail, telex or through SWIFT (the Society for Worldwide Interbank Financial Telecommunications). SWIFT is an automated inter-bank system for transfers and other communications.

Express International Money Transfer can be used to speed things up even more. The buyer's bank gives instructions to a bank in the exporter's country, either by coded cable, telex or by a priority SWIFT message. The cost of using the Express system needs to be weighed against the possible interest charge savings on an overdraft. And whether it's the buyer or the seller who foots the bill for using a quick payment method needs to be sorted out when the contract between them is being drawn up.

Case Story 11

When exporters can be caught over a barrel

A standard way of getting export contracts in some industries – construction and engineering particularly – is to put in a sealed bid. Bids are accompanied by 'bid bonds', documents negotiated through a bank which act as the buyer's guarantee that the seller's intentions are serious. But how serious is the buyer? is the question that sometimes needs asking.

In February 1985 a Middle Eastern company invited a firm of English engineering equipment suppliers to bid for a contract to specify and supply specially-manufactured control valves. The engineering company drew up the spec, asked the German manufacturers of those particular valves to name a price, and submitted bid and bid bond in the required 21 days.

The engineering firm heard nothing from the Middle East until a few days before the bid bond (valid for three months) was about to expire. A telex asked for it to be renewed for a further three months. The engineering firm was in a dilemma; no order had been received and bid bonds cost money. But the bid bond states quite clearly that, should the seller default on his quoted commitment, the buyer is entitled to a percentage of the price quoted (in this case two per cent). Anxious not to part with over £1,000 in this way, the engineering firm renewed the bond.

Five more times the engineering firm was asked to renew the bid bond and it still didn't know whether it would be awarded the contract or not.

In July 1986, fed up with the expense of the bid bonds and what it considered shoddy treatment from the customer, the engineering firm said it could no longer hold the quote at the prices stated unless there was some immediate action.

Two months later, the Middle Eastern company sent a purchase order and asked the firm to forward a 'performance bond' (the seller's guarantee that the firm will honour the contract. Should the firm renege, the buyer can claim a percentage of the quoted price — in this case ten per cent).

Although the engineering firm now had a firm order it couldn't fulfil it as the Middle Eastern company had not sent the promised letter of credit. This failed to arrive during the six month validity period of the performance bond, and, surprise, surprise, the Middle Eastern company asked for it to be renewed twice more (at a cost of around £145 each time).

Eventually, at the beginning of 1988, the letter of credit arrived, the order was processed and the engineering firm got paid. But what a lot of hassle and expense along the way, never mind the worry of whether the German valve suppliers would revalidate their quotation for the equipment.

If the engineering firm had taken out insurance to cover the bond from the ECGD, this situation wouldn't have arisen since ECGD builds in expiry dates on credit insurance policies. But — Catch 22 — the engineering firm couldn't have insured with ECGD since ECGD policies are limited to UK products, and the product in this case came from Germany.

Foreign currency or sterling?

When you quote a price for your goods to an overseas buyer, do you quote in sterling, in the customer's own currency or in another currency altogether? Traditionally, UK companies – especially long-established firms that remember the days when export trade was mainly to the Commonwealth – never consider quoting in any other currency but sterling and insist on payment in sterling.

But UK firms could well be losing orders by doing so. In most cases buyers prefer to use their own currency: it makes it easier for them to compare different price quotations, saves them the bother of converting, simplifies payment and avoids them bearing the currency risk. Buyers in some countries, eg the Middle East, always trade in US dollars.

With the sterling inflation rate so high over recent years, prices quoted in foreign currencies are more likely to remain stable for a reasonable period, too, so exporters might be saved the embarrassment of having to inform buyers frequently that the sterling price has risen yet again.

Selling in other currencies, of course, introduces a new problem: exchange rates yo-yo around and you need some protection against fluctuating rates wiping out some of your anticipated sterling profit. Here are the ways to cope with this:

- **Foreign forward exchange contracts.** You remove the risk of the exchange rate moving against you between the time the order is accepted and the time payment is due, by fixing with the bank the rate at which the bank will exchange the foreign currency into sterling at a specified time. If the exchange rate moves in your favour, that's just bad luck; if it moves against you, that's the bank's problem. This technique is normally used for protection of transaction exposure with a time scale up to 12 months. If the payment date is imprecise, the bank will allow the contract to be drawn down during a pre-determined period but this will be more expensive than a fixed date contract.

- **Foreign currency options.** This is a contract with the bank which gives you the right, but not the obligation, to sell the foreign currency you are expecting from your sale to the bank at a pre-determined exchange rate within a specified period, or on a specified date. It's not a commitment like a forward exchange contract, but an *option* – if the exchange rate has moved in your favour by the time you receive the money, you obviously won't want to exercise it (you will still have to pay the premium, though).

- **Foreign currency borrowings.** On the strength of your export contract you can borrow up to the same amount of foreign currency as stated in the contract. When your buyer pays you, you repay the loan with the borrowed money so eliminating the risk of exchange rate fluctuations. There will, of course, be interest to pay on the loan, but interest rates in other countries are often much lower than in the UK.

- **Currency accounts.** If you are doing a lot of international business in one particular country, consider opening a separate bank account in that country. This way, proceeds of sales are paid straight into this account and there is no need to convert into sterling.

Not only will you almost certainly be able to use the money more quickly perhaps to buy supplies, or to finance trips to see customers, but also while UK inflation is at a higher rate than that of many other industrialized countries, the advantage of having receivables in currencies which are depreciating at a slower rate than sterling is self-evident.

Countries compared

The table in Appendix B, compiled in 1990 by European credit management group Intrum Justita, sets out payment terms and debt collection procedures for eight European countries and the USA.

At the time of writing, Britain was one of the few European countries not to have introduced legislation to allow businesses the automatic right to levy interest charges for late payment of bills. This, however, will be rectified if an EC Directive currently working its way through the system is enforced.

Research by Intrum Justita also suggests that British companies are presently at a disadvantage with their European competitors because of Britain's poor payments discipline. British companies wait on average 78 days for their bills to be paid; Swedish and Norwegian companies wait just 48 days for debts to be settled; Danish firms wait 50 days while Dutch companies wait 52 days. Only Italian and French companies wait longer than British businesses – 90 and 108 days respectively – but since they quote 60-day payment terms, as opposed to the normal 30, they are still better off in relative terms. The EC Directive will make it a requirement for all EC businesses to pay for goods within 45 days, and there would be an automatic obligation to pay interest from the first day after the deadline.

Help for exporters

There is no shortage of help and advice for the exporter: banks, Chambers of Commerce, enterprise agencies, small firms' centres all provide it; there are also specialist governmental and other organizations listed below (see Appendix A for addresses):

- **The British Overseas Trade Board**. The overseas arm of the Department of Trade and Industry; there are regional offices throughout the country. The BOTB produces a range of booklets, many free, and provides the following services under the Export Initiative scheme: subsidized consultancy, market information enquiry service, market research studies, help with finding overseas representatives, an overseas status report service, help with fairs and promotions, missions and seminars overseas.
- **Export Market Information Centre**. Run by the DTI, this is an outstanding library for researching individual overseas markets and open to the public. The DTI also has a special telephone hotline (081–200 1992) for contacts and information on the Single European Market.
- **SITPRO (the Simplification of Trade Procedures Board)**. Sponsored by the BOTB, SITPRO works to simplify international trade procedures and documents and to provide more cost-effective methods of trading. Among other things, SITPRO sells standardized and simplified forms for export; provides information on simplified export procedures in a range of publications and leaflets; holds workshops and seminars and offers special software packages.
- **THE (Technical Help for Exporters)**. A department of the British Standards Institution and sponsored by the BOTB, THE offers specialist services to help exporters identify foreign technical requirements which may affect the design, installation or use of their products in overseas markets.

- **The Centre for European Business Information**. This is the London branch of a network of Euro Information centres throughout the EC and part of the government-sponsored Small Firms Service. The Centre contains information on EC business legislation; EC research and development programmes; company law; EC grants and loans; public sector contracts, competition policies, co-operative initiatives etc.
- **International Chamber of Commerce UK** and the **Institute of Export** are two other organizations which provide information and advice to exporters, the latter being a representative body for exporters which also organizes training courses and seminars.

9

Raising money

Most businesses need to raise finance at some time or another. It might be because the business is growing fast and finds it is underfinanced for what it wants to achieve; it might be to finance the purchase of a new asset or project; it might be to finance a projected cash shortfall or, more worryingly, to attempt to avert a cash crisis.

With proper budgetary controls and monitoring procedures in place (see Chapter 1), you should be able to spot a looming cash crisis in enough time to take corrective action. If a cash crisis occurs without warning, then the management of the company is probably to blame for having been too complacent – expecting the status quo to be maintained and thus not getting the forecasts right. The danger here is that there might not be enough time to save the business – if it's worth saving, ie still potentially profitable.

Raising more working capital to tide you over a difficult patch might be the only solution to a pending cash shortfall. This will only be possible, though, if the managers are able to demonstrate their ability to stem the cash losses and return the business to an even cash keel. And more money on loan is, of course, going to mean higher interest charges which may only worsen the situation. So, before deciding on this course of action, carry out a thorough review of your cash position and determine how much money can be released by a planned campaign of evasive action. Here's a checklist:

- Can you reduce the time taken to despatch the goods and invoice the customer?

- Can you collect money in from debtors faster?
- Are you paying creditors sooner than you need?
- If you are taking early payment discounts, should you change your policy for the present?
- Can you reduce your buying and re-ordering time for stock?
- Can you have a sale of stock to get rid of redundant/slow-moving lines?
- Can you put your prices up?
- If you are paying dividends should you cease while the crisis continues?
- Can you cut down your overhead costs?
- Can you manage with fewer employees?
- Is there spare plant or equipment which could be disposed of?

There might, of course, be no time to carry out this exercise, and however conscientiously you do so, you may still need to find additional funds.

What the lender wants to know

If you are borrowing money to avert a cash crisis, your chances of success will hinge on persuading the would-be lender that the crisis can be overcome. He will want to scrutinize your profit and cash flow forecasts and he will want to question you, the business managers, to make his own assessment of whether you have the ability to overcome the crisis.

You will need to have a credible explanation of how the crisis occurred and why it will not recur – if you can show that you've taken early and successful action to avoid previous crises, this should count in your favour.

Whatever the reason for the loan, lenders will look closely at your business's gearing (the ratio of money borrowed from outside sources – *debt capital* – to equity, or owners' capital including retained profits – *net worth*).

$$\text{Gearing ratio} = \frac{\text{debt capital}}{\text{net worth}}$$

Traditionally, 1:1 is the preferred ratio but financiers have become much more flexible in recent years. However, the higher the ratio, the greater the risk to the lender since a large proportion of external borrowings places the firm in deeper financial peril. The interest payments could become too great for the business to bear (which is what worries the lender) and the firm could go under if trade slumped.

Investors also often assess the risks in terms of interest cover:

$$\text{Interest cover} = \frac{\text{profit before interest and tax}}{\text{interest}}$$

This ratio shows the number of times the interest payable is covered by earnings. Lenders vary in the amount of cover they want to see, but, as a rough rule of thumb, the providers of unsecured loans would require cover of about five times.

Lenders will asses your competence as a business manager, your credibility with regard to the information supplied, your commitment to achieving business success and your response to the business environment in which you find yourself.

Writing a business plan

The preparation of business plans was something of a novelty for any firm other than the large corporations until the introduction of the Government Loan Guarantee Scheme in 1981 which required applicants to produce a plan. Now it's the main plank on which financiers assess businesses applying for term loans or equity finance. To stand a chance of success it thus needs to be well-worked out and well-presented. The reason you need the money should be explained in a way that's easy to understand. Vagueness is a besetting sin in business plans – lenders hate illogicality and want to know all the facts and figures.

This is what the plan should cover:

- **The business**: its age, history, status, where it's going and how it's going to get there.
- **The people running the business**: their experience and qualifications; their commitment to the enterprise both in terms of the cash the directors are prepared to put up and the amount of time they devote to it.
- **Premises**: size and costs.

- **Assets**: what there is and how it is financed.

- **Sales and marketing**: size of your marketplace, its trends and potential, the competition and its share of the market; orders in the pipeline; market research conducted; sales methods; distribution methods.

- **Trading performance**: results for the last three years with comments.

- **Financial position**: how you stand at the present moment regarding fixed assets, stock, debtors, creditors, net working capital, capital employed and how this is financed.

- **Future prospects**: cash flow forecasts and balance sheet projections for the next three years or so.

- **Financial requirements**: the amount of finance required with details of why you want it, when it will be needed and how you propose to fund it; how you plan to repay (if a loan) and what security you can put up; what size equity stake you are prepared to offer (if equity finance is what's required).

You can rarely dress up a poor idea or a bad business and persuade anyone to back it, but it's perfectly possible to present a good idea or a viable business so badly that it never gets off the financial starting blocks, which is why it's worth putting a good deal of thought and care into the business plan. In reality, though, the information lenders want differs little, if at all, from the information you need yourself. Business planning is essentially an exercise carried out for the benefit of the business – you can't identify future potential and possible pitfalls without planning ahead. The major banks now include sample business plans amongst their free literature, with advice on how to complete them.

Case Story 12

The Uncooperative bank

A successful high-tech company enjoyed an extremely amicable relationship with its local bank branch for nine years. Right from start-up, the bank manager had seen the potential of the business and supported it all the way along the line. The overdraft limit had been raised progressively from £20,000 to £135,000 which equalled the value of the owners' homes put

---

up as security.

Then, out of the blue, came a dictate from the bank's head office that the high-tech firm's account must be transferred to a special high-tech division set up by the bank in Mayfair. Both the firm and the bank manager strenuously resisted any move, but to no avail, and the account was transferred (for which the firm was charged a fee!)

After six months, the high-tech firm's new bank manager informed the directors that he saw the firm as 'very high risk' and required more security against the overdraft. Apart from putting up their homes, the directors had already given personal guarantees and the bank had taken a debenture on the company's assets – what more was there to give?

What the bank wanted was to be assigned all the high-tech company's intellectual property rights plus copies of the source code of the firm's specialized software package. If, said the bank manager, the firm was not prepared to do this, the overdraft would be immediately reduced to a mere £30,000.

No way was the high-tech firm prepared to release the right to its products. Why, asked the directors, should the bank be in possession of all the company secrets? It was akin to giving away the soul of the company itself.

What to do? Now for this firm it wasn't actually a great problem. The directors' annoyance at having their account moved so arbitrarily had led them to explore other banks, so they took up one of three offers made to them. The new bank not only maintained their £135,000 overdraft but charged ½ per cent less interest, didn't insist on personal guarantees and allowed the firm to factor its debts. But suppose this firm hadn't had another bank waiting in the wings?

Which finance for which purpose

There are several different ways of raising finance and which is right for which business depends on what the money is needed for. Fast-growing firms, for instance, are best advised to seek a permanent cash injection in the form of finance in return for a share stake since this way they improve their liquidity without incurring interest or repayment charges. It's also important to take out the right length of loan for the amount of time it is needed for. If, for instance, you wanted to acquire a piece of office equipment such as a photocopier it wouldn't be appropriate to finance it with a ten-year loan since you would still be paying for it long after the five or so year lifespan of the machine; you would take out a five-year loan or a five-year leasing contract (see Chapter 2). Similarly, you wouldn't acquire freehold premises with anything less than a long-term loan.

Terms of finance	What for	Methods of finance
Short-term (up to 3 years)	Stock, debtors, other working capital requirements, seasonal finance fluctuations, exporting	Trade creditors, overdrafts, short-term loans, factoring, invoice discounting, bills of exchange, letters of credit
Medium-term (3–7 years)	Fixed assets (plant, machinery, vehicles & other equipment), long-term working capital, developing a new product	Leasing, medium term loans, pension loanbacks
Long-term (7–20 years)	Permanent working capital, premises, major fixed assets, buying another business, expansion plans	Long-term loans, equity finance, mortgage loan, sale and leaseback

Overdrafts

Extending your overdraft facility is the first obvious route to try if you anticipate cash flow problems. It's simple to arrange and cheaper than most other forms of borrowing, with interest paid only on the outstanding daily balance. Do make sure, though, that the bank does not want to charge you an annual commitment fee on any unused part of the overdraft.

But don't push your luck where your overdraft is concerned, it's a facility that the bank has the power to control. At any time the bank can demand it to be reduced or repaid. And this isn't just in theory. Firms *are* asked to reduce their overdraft or threatened with the withdrawal of the facility altogether – often with disastrous results.

Term loans (short, medium, long)

These are a more formal borrowing arrangement than overdrafts; you pay an arrangement fee and you usually have to put up some security against the loan – a charge over all the assets of the business and, possibly, a personal guarantee which may have to be supported by a charge on personal assets, eg your home. Wherever possible, whether for overdrafts or loans, personal guarantees and charges on personal assets should be resisted and should certainly not be entered into without careful consideration.

The advantage of a loan, compared to an overdraft, is that normally it cannot be withdrawn on demand by the bank and is repayable over an agreed term of years. However, it is vital to read the small print of the loan agreement to ascertain in what circumstances the loan may become repayable on demand. This could happen if there is default in the terms of repayment or the value of the security given to the bank falls below the amount of the loan outstanding. You should appreciate that the value of any security can reduce sharply in times of recession, particularly when trading is difficult.

Interest charges on loans will be somewhere between three per cent and six per cent over bank base rate and you can sometimes choose between paying a fixed rate of interest (ie you pay the same rate throughout the life of the loan regardless of changes in the base rate) and a floating rate which varies with the base rate. A fixed rate makes cash flow forecasting and forward planning easier since you know exactly how much money you will be required to pay each month, but will inevitably cost more than a floating rate if interest rates continue downwards.

Who gives loans

When negotiating a loan you may be able to arrange to build in a capital repayment 'holiday'. This means that initially you only pay back the interest on the loan and repay the capital later (interest charges can be set off against income for Corporation Tax purposes). If you are using the money to purchase plant or equipment, this allows it to come fully into profit by the time the capital repayment programme starts.

All the banks offer business loans, and it's sensible to compare the interest charges and other fees they quote. Don't forget to include banks like the Co-op, TSB and Royal Bank of Scotland in your comparisons.

As well as their own loan schemes, the banks (and others) all lend under the *Government Loan Guarantee Scheme* which is designed to provide capital for small firms that have insufficient security to qualify for a normal bank loan. Loans up to £100,000 are available over a two to seven year period with the government guaranteeing 70 per cent of the loan for an annual premium. You can also opt for a capital repayment holiday of up to two years. However, you need to look carefully at the cost of the GLGS. Although the bank's rate of interest may be lower than for a normal loan (and the banks vary on the rate they levy), you have to add to this the premium to the government of one per cent annually on the 70 per cent of the loan it guarantees.

Another major provider of loans is 3i. Originally called ICFC, then Investors in Industry, 3i was formed in 1945 as a joint venture between the four major clearing banks and the Bank of England to provide the finance needed to stimulate business development after the War. It is now the largest provider of venture capital in the world, offering ordinary and convertible loans, and long-term finance in exchange for an equity stake.

3i deals with businesses of all sizes – the only size it is interested in is the future potential size of the business, not its existing size. Half of 3i's business is the straightforward provision of long-term loans to help established businesses undertake major projects, the other half is loans, converted preference shares and equity finance in a joint package, or just straight equity finance (see below). The loans and preference shares may well have conversion rights to enable 3i to swap them for an equity stake in the business if it becomes particularly successful and is either sold or floated on the stockmarket.

If your business is in one of Britain's Assisted Areas or a coal and steel closure area, find out from your local Department of Trade and Industry office whether you are eligible for a government grant or a loan from the EC or from BSC (Industry) Ltd, a subsidiary of British Steel Corporation. These loans carry low interest rates.

The Rural Development Commission offers limited loans to certain English country businesses; some local authorities operate loan schemes, as do the Welsh, Scottish and Ulster Development Agencies to businesses in their respective areas.

Factoring and invoice discounting

Factoring/invoice discounting are sources of finance especially designed to stop the blockages in your cash flow arteries. More and more firms are turning to factoring to keep their money moving, according to statistics from the Association of British Factors and Discounters. Companies are realizing it makes sense to optimize the use of one of their major resources – their trade debts. Factoring organizations advance money against these debts. They can also take over your credit control and debt collection.

When you use a factoring company you pass it all (or some) of your invoices. The factor pays you (either on receipt of the invoices or at an agreed date each month) a percentage of their value (up to 80 per cent). The factor then takes charge of your debt collection and passes the remainder of the invoice value to you when your customer pays (or on an agreed date).

How you pay

The factoring company charges you in two ways: first, it charges interest on the amount advanced (calculated from the date the advance was paid to the date the customer pays). Interest charges vary, but are usually in the region of two or three points above base rate.

Second it also charges you a fee for its services. This is determined by such things as the client company's sales volume; the market in which it operates and the number of invoices involved. The service charge can thus be anything from 0.5 per cent to four per cent of turnover.

Factoring can either be 'recourse' or 'non recourse'. The latter means the factor accepts responsibility for your bad debts and levies an additional charge for the credit insurance element. With recourse factoring, you foot the bill if your customer reneges on the debt. Although non-recourse is the safer option, be aware that the longer the debt remains unpaid the greater the amount of interest you pay the factor.

There is 'disclosed' and 'non-disclosed' factoring. Companies that consider a third party collecting their debts might upset relationships with customers can continue to receive payments in the normal way with a non-disclosed service. All payments, though, must be placed in a specially designated bank account under the joint control of factor and client. Interest rates are higher for a non-disclosed service.

Invoice discounting

Invoice discounting is a more limited version of factoring whereby the client remains responsible for his own debt collection and credit administration. The client sells all, or just a selection, of his sales invoices to the invoice discounter which advances him up to 75 per cent of their value and charges interest of around two per cent to five per cent above base rate.

Invoice discounting is usually provided on a recourse basis, although non-recourse invoice discounting can sometimes be arranged, and customers need never know you're using a third party since the service is confidential. Firms that already operate good credit control procedures and have few bad debts are suited to invoice discounting, and it could help firms with a widely variable cash flow because of seasonal trade or other reasons.

Both factoring and invoice discounting used to be considered services that were only used by large companies, but that is changing fast, particularly where factoring is concerned. It is eminently suitable for fast-growing smaller companies that need regular cash injections to maintain their liquidity, and it's this type of company that really benefits from having a ready-made credit control and collection department in the factoring company. It saves them staff and space and releases management time for other tasks.

The really big advantage of factoring is that it provides companies with the option of additional working capital without the need to find security or relinquish an equity stake in the business. It's ideal for firms that are sending out a large number of invoices each month to trade customers who are buying on short-term credit.

Export companies, where the problems of administration can be an even greater headache, could find factoring of particular benefit – although it's more expensive to factor export sales than UK sales. Some factors offer a package of export services to exporters selling on open account which, in addition to factoring, include such things as advice on trading terms in export markets; assistance with the resolution of disputes; elimination of the exchange risk when invoicing in foreign currency; swift transfer of funds to the UK; local knowledge of overseas buyers.

But factoring isn't cheap. You need to calculate carefully the anticipated costs against the possible savings factoring would make to your credit control operation, before you decide to go ahead. There are other disadvantages too: factoring companies are fussy about the debts they accept – they might not be the debts you want them to take. Also there is a loss of contact between you and your customers which may or may not worry you – factoring isn't flexible enough, for instance, for you to allow extended credit terms to certain customers whose goodwill you really value. If your bank has taken a charge on your assets you will need its permission to factor, and it might not allow this since debts constitute an important element of your assets.

Will a factoring company take you as a client anyway? They're quite choosy. They are only interested in soundly-managed companies which are growing profitably. They're looking for a volume of invoices with good minimum values. Most factoring companies want clients with a turnover of at least £75,000. Much larger turnovers are usually required for invoice discounting.

The 11 member companies of the Association of British Factors (see Appendix A) are responsible for most of the factoring business in the UK. All these factoring companies are part of large, international banking and financial groups. Smaller, more entrepreneurial factoring firms are now starting to appear on the scene; some of these combine factoring with other financial solutions for small fast-growing companies.

Case Story 13

Factoring made sense for this firm

A fast-growing software development business with £1m turnover was advised to factor its debts by the bank manager. The company needed money to expand and the bank convinced the firm that factoring would be a cheaper and better

---

option than extending the overdraft facility (the bank manager did stipulate, however, that the software firm should approach the bank's own associated factoring company!)

After careful vetting by the factor (only something like 25 per cent of firms that apply to factor their debts are taken on), the software company was signed up.

The factor advances this firm 70 per cent of the value of the invoices as soon as presented, and remits the remainder when the customers cough up (for domestic debts); after 60 days (for overseas accounts). As well as the three per cent interest over base charge, the software firm pays a 1–1.5 per cent commission on the turnover which goes through the factor for the service.

Not all the company's debts are factored. The factor wouldn't touch invoices for training fees or for maintenance charges (with these, the software firm now insists on payment in advance – no pay, no fix), nor would the factoring company agree to take invoices from the software firm's associated companies. All in all, about 60 per cent of turnover goes through the factoring firm.

But for this particular firm factoring has made a huge difference. With the factor taking over most of the debt chasing, the firm has been able to dispense with the services of a full-time credit controller, and the factor's efficient collection procedures mean that invoices are being paid in 30, rather than 90 days. The directors are delighted that they no longer have to worry about dunning debtors or taking people to court and can concentrate their energies on more important functions. What's more, there are no bad debts since the factor carries the total risk for the debts. The firm's customers, it should be said, are less delighted with the factor's tough, no-nonsense approach!

The amount of commission demanded by the factor is not seen as a problem by the directors; they reckon it's just about equivalent to what they would have been paying for an in-house credit control operation plus the increased interest charges on the extended overdraft. And the inevitable improvement in cash flow has allowed the software firm's expansion programme to go ahead by leaps and bounds. The problem they do foresee, though, is what happens when you

> want to stop factoring your debts? The factor is paying you so far in advance of when you would normally expect payment, that you'd need plenty of working capital to tide you over the three month or so gap of non-payment if you reverted back to normal collection procedures.

Bills of exchange

Bill financing is used extensively in import/export (see Chapter 8) trade but not a great deal for domestic transactions. There is no reason why it shouldn't be, and many people, including bank managers, believe it to be the ideal way to help the cash flow of smaller firms. Ironically, up until the latter half of the nineteenth century, the Bill Market was virtually the only market through which business could raise short-term finance – indeed the City was founded on the 'Bill of London' – but the spread of the clearing bank branch system and increasing reliance on the bank overdraft for working capital led to the decline of bills of exchange for internal trading transactions.

A bill of exchange is similar to a post-dated cheque. To use it as a method of payment, you send a written note to your customer, together with the goods you are supplying, stating that payment for the goods is to be made at a fixed, pre-determined date in the future. Your customer 'accepts' this by signing it, and returns it to you. You can then sell the bill at a discount to a financial institution and so receive cash for the sale immediately.

Bills are normally drawn for periods of 91 days (although one-month, two-month and six-month bills can be issued). The market in bills is controlled by the City's discount houses and by the clearing and merchant banking community. This is the formula for calculating the discount charged:

$$\text{Discount} = \frac{\text{capital sum} \times \text{interest rate}}{100} \times \frac{\text{no of days the bill has to run}}{365}$$

So, for example, a £100,000 bill discounted at 10½ per cent, say, on 15 October and due on 15 December:

$$\text{Discount} = £100,000 \times \frac{10\frac{1}{2}}{100} \times \frac{61}{365} = £1,754.79$$

The daily 'going' rates for bills of exchange are published under Money Markets in the *Financial Times* under the headings *Eligible Bank* (bills) and *Fine Trade* (bills). 'Fine' trade bills are trade bills which are backed by credit insurance. The discount rates on trade bills which aren't covered by insurance will be higher and will depend on the creditworthiness of the buyer and seller, and you, the seller, will be responsible for paying the debt if your buyer defaults.

Bank bills are those where the bill of exchange is drawn upon the bank and is 'accepted' by the bank (for a commission). Here, the bank takes full responsibility for the debt so credit insurance for bad debts is not necessary. 'Eligible' bank bills are those that have been accepted by a recognized bank – a clearing bank, a discount house, a merchant bank member of the Accepting Houses Committee, some British overseas banks and certain foreign banks.

As a source of short-term financing, bills of exchange offer several advantages: the discount rate is usually competitive with the interest rate on overdrafts; it allows you to calculate accurately the cost of financing a transaction as the discount rate is fixed and not subject to interest rate fluctuations; and it frees your overdraft facilities for other purposes.

Equity finance

Most businesses are financed by a combination of owners' funds, borrowed money, trade credit and retained profits (if any), but there is another financing route open to the limited liability company (but not sole traders and partnerships): that of issuing additional shares to raise money from third parties not associated with the business owners.

Business owners frequently jib at the idea of parting with a share stake in return for an injection of capital. They fear they will lose control of the business and resent the fact that if the shares go up in value because of their hard work, someone else stands to reap part of the reward. However, a company can only grow at the rate at which its funding base is growing and if your company can't expand without more cash, equity finance may be the only answer, being interest free and requiring no capital repayments. Don't look at it as parting with shares, see it as selling to an outsider a part share of the business as a means of achieving objectives which couldn't be realized in the timescale required without the injection of that outside capital. Ask yourself this: is it better to have 100 per cent of a very small cake or 75 per cent of a cake that's twice the size?

But it isn't right for every sort of business. Providers of equity finance (also called risk capital, venture capital, development capital) classify businesses into two types: *Proprietorial*, those concerned mainly with providing a decent living for their owners, and *Entrepreneurial*, those that intend to make it to the big time. The risk/return ratio which financiers are seeking (between 30 per cent and 40 per cent compound annually) means they are much more interested in backing the latter, and, for those, there is plenty of money around – financiers complain that their problem is finding the right businesses to back.

Although an equity cash injection means the company may lose some flexibility in the way it conducts its business affairs, particularly regarding significant capital expenditure and remuneration levels for directors and shareholders, overall control is never lost because professional lenders only require a minority stake – usually no more than 30 per cent. Equity finance can have other advantages too over loan finance: it will almost certainly be cheaper while the business is growing and can bring with it the skills and expertise the business owner lacks in the shape of a non-executive director on the company's board. It can also enhance the firm's status and extend its borrowing power further – commercial lenders are likely to view an increased shareholding favourably.

Over the last ten years the supply of risk capital has increased quite dramatically (there is now more available per head in the UK than in the USA), although there has traditionally been something of a problem for firms only needing to raise small amounts – under £100,000, say – since the main risk capital providers prefer to deal in larger amounts because of the relative costs of appraising/selecting proposals and the subsequent monitoring of investments.

However, new funds are now starting up to lend smaller amounts to businesses in a particular geographical area or a particular industrial sector, and there are individuals looking for unquoted companies to back.

Case Story 14

Successful equity financing

A company formed to manufacture small quantities of own-label products for hairdressing salons and independent chemists that wished to sell their own brands, exhausted it. own funds and set about looking for a private individual who would invest in the business and join it as a working director.

A feature article about the cosmetics company in *Venture Capital Report* (a publication that exists to match up investors and companies) produced seven likely candidates. The cosmetics company MD selected a candidate with marketing expertise.

The private investor put in £15,000 in return for 25 per cent of the equity and a seat on the board. He immediately set about changing the company's corporate image and initiating a £10,000 advertising campaign.

At the time he joined the company there were 26 customers buying 41 product lines. Six months after his arrival the number of customers had jumped to 120 and turnover was up five-fold on the previous year with an estimated fourfold rise the following year. The company was making a loss when the investor came but showed profits of nearly £100,000 at the end of the investor's first year.

Individual backers

In 1983, the government, with the aim of providing a real source of risk capital for the fledgling businesses it then saw as the bedrock of Britain's future economy, introduced the **Business Expansion Scheme** which offers generous tax relief for individuals who buy shares in young, unquoted companies. Individuals can invest from £500 to £40,000 for a minimum of five years and for a maximum of 30 per cent of the equity of a company and claim tax relief at the marginal rate of income tax. Thus, a top-rate (40 per cent) taxpayer purchasing at the upper investment limit would be able to claim back £16,000, and the net cost of the share purchase of £40,000 would be £24,000.

Two of its rules, though, make the Business Expansion Scheme less attractive than it might have been. The most logical people to pump money into a company – the directors, their immediate family, and the employees – are not eligible for tax relief under BES, and investors under BES are not allowed to be remunerated for any work they do for the company which rules out a lot of people who want involvement.

There is also the very real problem of finding an individual investor. Local stockbrokers, solicitors, accountants, enterprise agencies might be able to put you in touch with one. The business-to-business pages of the national daily and Sunday papers sometimes contain advertisements (or you could advertise your-self).

Two less hit-and-miss methods of tracking down individuals who might invest in your company are through LINC, the financial marriage bureau run by the local enterprise agencies, and through the magazine *Venture Capital Report*. These investors, though, will not necessarily be people looking to invest under BES. They are quite likely to be people who want to put their time and expertise to good use by sitting on the board of the company(s) they take an interest in, and be financially rewarded for doing so which, as stated above, the BES rules don't allow.

LINC (address in Appendix A) introduces firms to potential investors by means of a monthly bulletin (cost of an entry £50). This carries brief descriptions of firms seeking finance and is sent to all the potential investors on the LINC database. Firms also sometimes attend 'investor meetings' where they present their case for finance to a group of assembled investors.

Venture Capital Report (address in Appendix A) prepares feature articles on companies wishing to attract investors, for a fee plus a percentage of any money raised. The monthly publication goes out to around 1,000 investors – private individuals, banks and other financial institutions and venture capital companies.

VCR is quite careful about choosing the companies it includes. The editor will want to interview you and examine your proposal, and an article will only be written if your scheme is considered viable.

Funds and institutions

The problem with the Business Expansion Scheme of matching wealthy people with needy businesses, combined with the very real risk involved for individuals investing in young unquoted companies, has led to most BES money being channelled into specially-created business expansion *funds*. These funds, managed by people mainly from the merchant banking etc world, pool investors' resources and the fund managers select companies they consider worth investing in from the applications submitted.

Since the fund managers have a duty to maximize tax allowances for investors as well as ensuring that their money is secure, and since the fund's administration costs don't vary substantially between a £10,000 or £100,000 investment, the funds have tended to favour companies with a proven track record that need a substantial cash injection.

There are, however, some funds and syndicates which do lend amounts under £50,000 – you'll find them listed, along with other providers of small amounts of risk capital, in *Risk Capital for Small Firms: a Guidebook and Directory* published on behalf of the Small Business Research Trust by Barclays Bank.

There are now well over 100 sources of risk capital, ranging from the clearing banks, 3i, the biggest provider of venture capital in the world, and mentioned above under term loans, to merchant banks, pension funds and other financial institutions.

These organizations differ in the arrangement fees they take for backing a company and in the amount of equity stake required – anything from one per cent to 49 per cent. Some providers are only interested in certain types of business, and several will provide loan finance combined with equity funding.

Many providers insist on appointing one of their people to your board of directors. They claim it's a way of adding value to the company, but it's actually just as much a part of protecting their investment. However, many companies do find non-executive directors a real boon. They find it useful to have an outsider to bounce ideas off, especially if his skills are complementary to those of the business owners. He might, too, have valuable contacts with other organizations which could lead to potential new customers or suppliers.

3i doesn't believe in putting one of its own people on a customer company's board, preferring to avoid the conflicts that can arise from playing the dual role of investor and director. It has, though, set up a separate 'Associate Director Resource' – a list of non-executive directors around the country who have worked with 3i – which 3i customers can access if they think a non-executive director would benefit the business.

Two sources for discovering the names and addresses of venture capital providers are:

Venture Capital 1990 free from Stoy Hayward; *Directory 1991* from the British Venture Capital Association (addresses in Appendix A).

Pension loanbacks

Where a firm runs a pension scheme, this can be used to release money for use back in the business. This could be for working capital, office improvements or the purchase of business equipment and vehicles. A pension fund can also buy non-industrial buildings and rent them to the company at a commerical rent. Often the interest and other terms give this type of loan an edge over traditional bank lending.

At the time of writing (January 1991) there is no limit on the amount that 'large' schemes (with 12 or more members) can loan to the sponsoring company. Loans from small self-administered schemes are restricted to half the amount currently in the scheme and must be at a commercial rate of interest (normally bank base rate plus three per cent) and for a specific purpose.

All this is likely to change during 1991. New rules announced by the Inland Revenue will limit loans in the first two years from small schemes to 25 per cent of the assets of the scheme. This will increase to 50 per cent after two years as at present.

However, if any of the members of the scheme, or their immediate family, do not control 20 per cent of the voting rights in the company, or if not all of the members are trustees, loans and other forms of 'self-investment' (including property leased back to the business) will be limited to five per cent of the scheme's assets. This last rule will apply to all schemes, small and large, when regulations expected under the Social Security Act 1990 become effective. Check with an accountant whether these new rules are in force if you are contemplating a pension loanback.

Sale and leaseback

If you own the freehold of your property, or a long lease, and need to raise additional funds, you may be able to receive cash to the value of the property by selling it to a financial institution such as an insurance company or pension fund that will grant you a lease to continue occupying the premises.

You will probably need to have a good profit track record, though, before a lender will be interested, and you will have to foot the bill for all the expenses involved in doing it. You also forgo the potential rise in the value of the property and may be subjected to restrictive covenants in the lease.

Mortgage loan

This operates in much the same way as an ordinary mortgage. The money borrowed is used to buy the freehold or long leasehold on the business premises. The property then acts as security for the loan, with regular repayments made up of interest charges and principal paid to the lender.

What to do with surplus cash

It is claimed that many large companies make more profit from the astute management of their surplus cash than they do from the sale of their products. British Leyland, for instance, at one time made a loss from manufacturing cars but a substantial profit from its money market dealings located in Switzerland.

Unfortunately, many smaller businesses are not profitable enough to include surplus cash among their current assets, relying as they often have to on the overdraft for all cash needs. However, if the good housekeeping and other procedures outlined in the preceding chapters are adhered to, extra cash would be the logical outcome. It is sensible to hold reserves of cash, when possible, since it provides protection against cash flow uncertainty, or against the overdraft being reduced or recalled, and allows you to take advantage of new opportunities for making profit.

Whether or not you can turn cash management into a profit centre in its own right will depend on both the amount of surplus cash you have to play with and how cleverly you invest it.

Whenever there is surplus cash in the business it's foolish to let it lie idle in a non-interest paying account if it could be earning interest for you in some other way. It's sensible to forecast the closing balance of your current account each day, and if the account has a significant credit balance transfer all or some of this to a deposit account held with the same bank. The transfer can probably be arranged by telephone and confirmed in writing (it's not worth transferring, of course, if the interest receivable will be lower than the charges for making the transfer).

Ordinary deposit accounts, though, don't yield very high rates of interest and businesses which regularly have fairly substantial amounts of surplus cash should look for ways to get a higher return on the money.

When considering surplus cash investments you need to think about:

- **Maturity**: how quickly you want to withdraw the money. This varies from overnight to a year or more. Many companies with spare cash know that the money will be needed back in the business fairly soon to meet payments out, or to finance new projects, so it's important to ensure that the withdrawal time for that proportion of the money fits in with the requirements of the business.
- **Security**: how much of a risk you are prepared to take – the greater the risk, the higher the rewards.
- **Yield**: the rate of interest you will receive.
- **Tax**: the tax implications of the different types of investment in short-term funds – returns should always be measured in after-tax income.

The Money Market

More favourable interest rates are available by dealing on the Money Market. This is not a physical marketplace, it's the name given to the financial telephone trading which takes place in the City of London. The money-market dealers, generally located in the head offices of the major banks, aim to make their profit from the margin between the borrowing and lending rates for sterling.

You deposit your surplus cash on the money market for periods ranging from overnight to a year or more. In return you are paid interest. The interest is calculated according to the number of days elapsed on a 365-day basis. Thus, a deposit of £1 million placed on 1 March and maturing on 5 March at an interest rate of ten per cent would earn interest of:

$$£1,000,000 \times \frac{10}{100} \times \frac{4}{365} = £1,095.89$$

(The formula is $p \times \frac{i}{100} \times \frac{n}{365}$

where p is the principal amount, i is the interest rate, n the number of elapsed days.)

As well as offering quite a number of different types of deposit, negotiable instruments such as bills of exchange, treasury bills and certificates of deposit are traded on the Money Market. Negotiable instruments are a good form of liquid investment if you are not sure how long funds will be available for since they can be resold whenever cash is needed. However, price on resale fluctuates with interest rates – so if you sell when rates are high you may incur a loss.

Treasury bills (from £5,000 upwards) are very safe short-term investments as both capital and investment are guaranteed by the government. They have a maturity of between one week and one year.

Certificates of deposit are interest-bearing deposits with the major banks. Interest is paid annually or on maturity if less than twelve months. The period of maturity varies between three months and five years but you can sell them at any time. The minimum face value of a CD is £50,000.

Playing the Money Market directly (or through a broker) is really a game for businesses with at least £250,000 to invest. However, for businesses with less surplus cash, the major banks operate money market deposit accounts, the rate of interest being agreed for each transaction. The minimum level of these deposits can be as low as £1,000 for those at seven day notice and £50,000 for deposits at call.

Your local clearing bank branch will be able to arrange for you to place funds in a variety of deposit accounts, or for the funds to be placed directly with its head office dealing room. The advantage to you of going through your local branch is that administration and settlement can be handled by the branch on your behalf.

Companies that aren't likely to require their surplus cash back at short notice can invest in the stock market. Shares can, of course, be sold at any time to provide instant cash but this rather defeats the object of the exercise. And you might even lose money if any profit doesn't exceed dealer costs, or share prices take a nose dive and you need your money out.

A portfolio of short maturity gilts is a safe way to invest. For a higher capital gain, but a commensurate amount of risk, think about a portfolio of 'blue chip' company shares (companies where the ability to pay dividends is assured). There are still higher yields to be had, but the highest yields of all are offered by companies that the market doesn't believe can continue their dividends at the same level. The sensible corporate investor buys into companies that offer a high yield by way of dividends, but are well covered by profits.

If you have any competitors who are quoted on the stock market, why not buy shares in them too? This will enable you to receive a copy of their annual accounts, information about any acquisitions they make and, if you wish, you can attend their company meetings.

Appendix A

Addresses

Aldwark Management Training Ltd, The Conference Suite, 106 Micklegate, York YO1 1JX (0904 647728)

Association of British Factors and Discounters, Hind Court, 147 Fleet Street, London EC4A 4BU (071–353 1213)

Association of Professional Computer Consultants, Penn House, 16 Peterborough Road, Harrow, Mddx HA1 2YN (081–422 6460)

Bankruptcy Search Room, Commercial Union House, Martineau Square, Birmingham B24 UZ (021–233 4808)

The Brain Exchange, AIESEC Great Britain Ltd, 26 Phipp Street, London EC2A 4NR (071–739 9847)

The British Overseas Trade Board, 1 Victoria Street, London SW1H 0ET (071–215 7877)

British Venture Capital Association, 3 Catherine's Place, London SW1E 6DX (071–233 5212)

Centre for European Business Information, Small Firms Service, 11 Belgrave Road, London SW1V 1RB (071–828 6201)

The Centre for Interfirm Comparison, Capital House, 48 Andover Road, Winchester, Hampshire SO23 7BH (0962 844144)

Chartered Institute of Marketing, Moor Hall, Cookham, Berks SL6 9QH (06285 24922)

Chartered Institute of Management Accountants, 63 Portland Place, London W1N 4AB (071–637 2311)

CMTC Management Centre, Woodland Grange, Leamington Spa, Warwickshire CV 32 6RN (09263 36621)

Companies Registration Office, Crown Way, Cardiff CF4 3UZ (0222 388588); and London Search Room, 55 City Road, London

EC1Y 1BB (071–253 9393)
Companies Registration Office (Scotland), 102 George Street, Edinburgh EH2 3DJ (031–225 5774)
Cranfield Institute of Technology, Cranfield, Bedford MK4 0AL (0234 751122)
The Credit Services Association, The Grange, 1 Hoole Road, Chester CH2 3NQ (0244 319912)
Department of Trade and Industry Regional Offices
   North East: Stangate House, 2 Groat Market, Newcastle-upon-Tyne NE1 1YN (091–232 4722)
   North West: Sunley Towers, Piccadilly Plaza, Manchester M1 4BA (061–838 5000)
   Yorkshire and Humberside: 25 Queen Street, Leeds LS1 2TW (0532 443171)
   East Midlands: Severns House, 20 Middle Pavement, Nottingham NG1 7DW (0602 506181)
   West Midlands: Ladywood House, Stephenson Street, Birmingham B2 4DT (021 623 4111)
   South West: The Pithay, Bristol BS1 2PB (0272 272666)
   London: Bridge Place, 88–9 Eccleston Square, London SW1V 1PT (071–627 7800)
   South East (Cambridge): The Westbrook Centre, Milton Road, Cambridge CB4 1YG (0223 461939)
   South East (Reading): 40 Caversham Road, Reading, Berkshire RG1 7EB
   Scotland: Industry Department for Scotland, Alhambra House, 45 Waterloo Street, Glasgow G2 6AT (041 248 2855)
   Wales: Welsh Office Industry Department, Treforest Industrial Estate, Pontypridd, Mid-Glamorgan CF37 5UR (0222 823185)
   N. Ireland: Dept of Economic Development, Netherleigh House, Massey Avenue, Belfast BT4 2JT (0232 63244)
   Single European Market Hotline: 081–200 1992
Dun & Bradstreet Ltd, Holmers Farm Way, High Wycombe, Bucks HP12 4UL (0494 422000)
Electricity Council, 30 Millbank, London SW1P 4RD (071–834 2333)
Energy Efficiency Office, Eland House, Stag Place, London SW1E 5DH (071–273 0690)
Energy Systems Trade Association, PO Box 16, Stroud, Glos GL5 5EB (045 387 3568)
Engineering Industries Association, 16 Dartmouth Street, London

SW1H 9BL (071–222 2367)
Enterprise Initiative *contact* your DTI regional office
The Equipment Leasing Association, 18 Upper Grosvenor Street, London W1X 9PB (071–491 2783)
Export Credits Guarantee Department, PO Box 272, Export House, 50 Ludgate Hill, London EC4M 7AY (071–382 7000)
Export Market Information Centre, 1 Victoria Street, London SW1H 0EH (071–215 5444)
3i, 91 Waterloo Road, London SE1 8XP (071–928 7822)
ICC Business Information, Field House, 72 Old Field Road, Hampton, Mddx TW12 2HQ (081–783 0922)
The Institute of Credit Management, Easton House, Easton-on-the-Hill, Stamford, Lincs PE9 3NZ (0780 56777)
Institute of Export, Export House, 64 Clifton Street, London EC2A 4HB (071–247 9812)
Institute of Purchasing and Supply, Easton House, Easton-on-the-Hill, Stamford, Lincs PE9 3NZ (0780 56777)
International Chamber of Commerce UK, 14–15 Belgrave Square, London SW1X 8PS (071–823 2811)
Intrum Justita Limited, Warwick House, Birmingham Road, Stratford-upon-Avon, Warwickshire CV37 0BP (0789 415181)
Jordan & Sons Ltd, 21 St Thomas Street, Bristol BS1 6JS (0272 230600)
LINC, 4 Snow Hill, London EC1A 2BS (071-236 3000)
The Local Enterprise Development Unit, LEDU House, Upper Galwally, Belfast BT8 4TB (0232 491031)
Management Consultants Association, 11 West Halkin Street, London SW1X 8JL (071–235 3897)
Mobile Training and Exhibitions Ltd, Temple Close, Sibford Gower, Banbury, Oxon OX15 5RX (029 578 8115)
MSS Services Ltd, PO Box 31, Worthing, West Sussex (0903 34755)
National Training Index, 1st Floor, 25/26 Poland Street, London W1V 3DB (071–494 0596)
Purchasing Management Services, Rose Villa, Main Street, Alne, York YO6 2HS (0347 3606)
Registry Trust Ltd, 173/175 Cleveland Street, London W1P 5PE (071–380 0133)
Royal Institution of Chartered Surveyors, 12 Great George Street, Parliament Square, London SW1P 3AD (071–222 7000)
Rural Development Commission, 141 Castle Street, Salsibury,

Wiltshire SP1 3TP (0722 336255)

Scanmark, Buckinghamshire College of Higher Education, 6 Newland Park, Gorelands Lane, Chalfont St Giles, Bucks HP8 4AD (02407 4441)

Scottish Development Agency, Rosebury House, Haymarket Terrace, Edinburgh EH12 5EZ (031–337 9595)

Shaws Linton Courses Ltd, 35 Market Place, Wantage, Oxon OX12 8AE (02357 688555)

SITPRO (The Simplification of Trade Procedures Board), Venture House, 29 Glasshouse Street, London W1R 5RG (071–287 3525).

Stoy Hayward, 8 Baker Street, London W1M 1DA (071–486 5888)

Technical Help for Exporters, Linford Wood, Milton Keynes, MK14 6LE (0908 220022)

Ulster Development Agency *see* The Local Enterprise Development Board

Venture Capital Report, Boston Road, Henley-on-Thames, Oxon RG9 1DY (0491 579999)

Welsh Development Agency, Pearl House, Greyfriars Road, Cardiff CF1 3XX (0222 222666)

Appendix B

International payments and collections

The diversity of legislation and business culture in Europe has produced a widely varying picture of debt from country to country. Contractual terms range from 30 days to 120 days and overdue days show the same degree of disparity.

The chart below shows the average number of days credit allowed and the average number of days it takes for debts to be paid in a number of European countries.

The guide overleaf shows how Great Britain compares with seven of its EC trading partners and the USA where debt collection procedures are concerned. Both these tables are taken from information compiled by international credit management group, Intrum Justita.

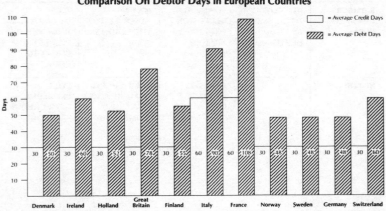

Comparison On Debtor Days in European Countries

HOW TO MAINTAIN A POSITIVE CASH FLOW

	■ BELGIUM	■ DENMARK	■ FRANCE	■ GERMANY
NORMAL TERMS OF PAYMENT:	30–60 DAYS NET	DOMESTIC: 30 DAYS EXPORT: 60 DAYS	30–90 DAYS NET	30 DAYS
CASH DISCOUNT:	10 DAYS 2%	10 DAYS 2–3%, NOT USUAL	IMMEDIATE PAYMENT 1–2.5%	COMMON IN SOME INDUSTRIES
INTEREST ON OVERDUE ACCOUNTS:	IF AGREED 12%, OTHERWISE MAX. 8%	BANK RATE + 6% LEGAL.	NORMALLY 15%	BANK RATE + 6%.
NORMAL DEMAND ROUTINES:	2–3 REMINDERS. 15–30 DAYS	2 REMINDERS AFTER 2–4 WEEKS.	2 REMINDERS. 24 DAYS–30 DAYS	3 REMINDERS. INTERVALS 2–3 WEEKS. LAST ONE BY LAWYER
COMMON COLLECTION METHODS:	DEMAND LETTER, PHONECALL, STREET COLLECTORS	LAWYERS MONOPOLY: THEY MUST WRITE COLLECTION DEMANDS	DEMAND LETTER, PHONE-CALLS	DEMAND LETTER, PHONECALL, LEGAL ACTION
COURT ACTION: LIMITATION OF TIME	IN GENERAL 30 YEARS.	CONSUMERS: 5 YEARS. RETAIL: 5 YEARS. JUDGEMENTS: 20 YEARS	CONSUMERS: 30 YEARS. RETAIL: 10 YEARS	CONSUMERS: 2 YEARS. RETAIL: 4 YEARS. JUDGEMENTS: 30 YEARS
POWER OF ATTORNEY:		NOT NEEDED	NOT NECESSARY. HOWEVER COMMON PRACTICE	ALWAYS NEEDED
REIMBURS-EMENT OF COSTS:	ALL COSTS TO BE PAID BY THE DEBTOR	LEGAL AND COLLECTION COSTS TO BE PAID BY DEBTOR	MAY BE ALLOWED BY THE COURTS	TO BE PAID BY DEBTOR, HOWEVER IT VARIES FROM COURT TO COURT
NOTES:		PAYMENTS ARE MADE BY SWIFT	COMMERCIAL DAMAGE CAN BE REIMBURSED. TRANSFER TIMES SLOW	STILL PROBLEMS WITH CHEQUE PAYMENTS.

■ GREAT BRITAIN	■ ITALY	■ NETHER-LANDS	■ SPAIN	■ U.S.A.
DOMESTIC: 30 DAYS. EXPORT 30–90 DAYS	BETWEEN 60–90 DAYS.	30 DAYS.	30–90 DAYS NET	30 DAYS
UNUSUAL	DOMESTIC PAYMENT 3–4%	UNUSUAL	UNUSUAL	10 DAYS 2.5%
DIFFICULT WITHOUT A CONTRACT. LEGAL ACTION 15%	PRESENT 5% PER ANNUM. IF CONTRACTS HIGHER RATES	SELDOM CHARGED. BANK INTEREST 9–12%	BANK RATE + 2% (10%) TODAY. HIGHER IF AGREED	NOT COMMON UNLESS AGREED
2–3 REMINDERS 14–30–60 DAYS	2–3 REMINDERS	2–4 REMINDERS	2–4 REMINDERS DURING AN INTERVAL OF 1–2 MONTHS	2–4 REMINDERS + PHONECALLS.
DEMAND LETTERS. PHONE-CALLS. LEGAL ACTION	REGISTERED MAIL. PHONECALLS. LEGAL ACTION	DEMAND LETTER. PHONECALL. LEGAL ACTION	DEMAND LETTERS. PHONECALLS. LEGAL ACTION	DEMAND LETTER. MANY PHONE-CALLS. LEGAL ACTION
6 YEARS FROM WHEN ACTION WAS INITIATED	10 YEARS. IN CASE OF JUDGEMENT: NO LIMITATION OF TIME	30 YEARS. SHORTER IN CERTAIN INDUSTRIES	GENERALLY: 15 YEARS. OTHER PERIODS ALSO EXIST	GENERALLY 7 YEARS
NOT NEEDED	SPECIAL FORMS ARE NEEDED AND ALWAYS NECESSARY	NOT NEEDED	ALWAYS NEEDED	NOT NECESSARY. COMMON IN LEGAL CASES
TO BE PAID BY DEBTOR WHEN LEGAL ACTION IS TAKEN	INJUNCTION PROCEDURE – PARTLY. EXECUTION COSTS – FULLY	IF A JUDGEMENT IS RECEIVED 15%	AFTER COURT ACTION TO BE PAID BY DEBTOR	NOT RECOVER-ABLE UNLESS A CONTRACT
VERY CONSERVA-TIVE BANKING SYSTEM	BANKING SYSTEM VERY SLOW AND INEFFICIENT.	BANKING SYSTEM IS CLEAR AND EFFECTIVE	BANKING SYSTEM VERY SLOW AND INADEQUATE	CHEQUE PAYMENTS NORMAL. SWIFT BECOMING COMMON

Index

INDEX

INDEX